C# & C++
Programming Unlocked

[7 IN 1] Conquer Coding Fears, Master Game & Mobile/IoT
Development, and Transform into an IT Expert with this Course
Guide for Budding Coders to Industry Pros

By

Andrew Sullivan

© Copyright 2023 - All rights reserved

ANDREW SULLIVAN

⚝ HERE IS YOUR FREE GIFT!

👇 SCAN HERE TO DOWNLOAD IT FOR FREE

1. **Master the Intricacies of C# & C++:** Whether you're aiming for a top-tier game development role or just looking to elevate your coding prowess, this cheat sheet is your key to unlocking the complexities of two of the industry's most sought-after languages.

2. **Stay Ahead in the Tech Race:** Feeling overwhelmed by the rapid pace of tech trends? Our cheat sheet is meticulously crafted to ensure you're not just keeping up, but leading the way. Prepare to stand out in a sea of expert programmers!

3. **From Novice to Authority:** This cheat sheet is more than just a guide; it's a roadmap to achieving your aspirations. Transform your fears of underperformance into a legacy of technical excellence and mentorship in the programming world!

👇 SCAN HERE TO DOWNLOAD IT FOR FREE

Table of Contents

C# & C++ PROGRAMMING UNLOCKED

C# & C++ PROGRAMMING UNLOCKED

Introduction

In the ever-evolving landscape of programming, the languages of C# and C++ have stood the test of time, empowering developers to create powerful, efficient, and versatile applications. As we delve into the pages of this comprehensive guide, *C# & C++ Programming Unlocked*, we embark on a journey through the intricacies of these languages, uncovering their vast potential and unlocking the doors to a world of endless possibilities.

Over the past decades, the significance of programming languages has grown exponentially, mirroring the changing demands of industries and the evolving needs of users. In this context, our goal is not only to equip you with a deep understanding of C# and C++ but also to provide you with the tools to excel in various domains, from game development and systems programming to web applications and scientific computing. We recognize that each reader comes with unique aspirations and interests, and our aim is to cater to a diverse audience, whether you are a beginner taking your first steps into the programming world or an experienced developer looking to expand your skill set.

Throughout the pages of this book, we follow a carefully crafted roadmap, divided into seven distinct sections, each focusing on a specific aspect of C#, C++, or their harmonious combination. Starting with the essential foundations in *Book 1 - C# Programming: The Essential Guide for Beginners*, we gently immerse ourselves in the fundamentals of C# syntax, data types, decision-making, and object-oriented programming. With clarity and precision, we lay the groundwork for your coding journey, ensuring a strong footing as you progress.

Continuing the expedition, *Book 2 - C# Programming: Intermediate Techniques and Frameworks* propels us forward, exploring data structures, algorithms, advanced object-oriented programming, and the practical applications of C# frameworks and libraries. Here, we venture into the realm of web development, gaining insights into building web applications with ASP.NET and mastering the art of performance optimization. Along the way, we engage in a comprehensive project, developing an inventory management web application using ASP.NET, allowing you to apply newfound knowledge to a real-world scenario.

In *Book 3 - C# Programming: Advanced Concepts and Industry Practices*, we ascend to new heights, unraveling the intricacies of delegates, events, LINQ, web design, component-based programming, and responsive design. We delve into the world of software engineering, exploring design patterns, testing strategies, and professional project development. Through hands-on experiences and projects, we showcase the power of C# in crafting robust enterprise solutions and Unity games, preparing you for the challenges of the professional realm.

Switching gears, *Book 4 - C++ Programming: A Practical Introduction* ushers us into the realm of C++, a language renowned for its performance and low-level programming capabilities. We embark on a comprehensive journey, acquainting ourselves with the fundamentals of C++, including variables, operators, pointers, and object-oriented programming. We gain practical insights into real-world applications of C++ and lay the groundwork for further exploration.

Book 5 - C++ Programming: Mastering Complex Structures and Database Management propels us deeper into the realm of C++, where we unlock the power of advanced features such as templates, the Standard Template Library (STL), graphical libraries, and database management. Here, we uncover the potential of C++ in high-performance projects, industrial IoT, and microcontroller firmware, preparing you to navigate the dynamic programming landscape and embrace emerging trends.

Book 6 - C# and C++: Bridging the Gap explores the interoperability of these languages, highlighting their combined strength in data analysis, high-performance applications, and practical projects. We witness the synergy between C# and C++ as they converge to tackle complex challenges, equipping you with versatile tools to address real-world scenarios and maximize your coding prowess.

Finally, in *Book 7 - C# and C++: Career Preparation and Beyond*, we focus on the bigger picture, preparing you for the exciting possibilities that lie ahead. We delve into the job market for C# and C++ developers, discussing certifications, essential skills, resume building, and interview strategies. Moreover, we examine industry trends and guide you on the path of continuous learning and growth, equipping you with the knowledge and resources to stay ahead in this ever-evolving field.

As we embark on this journey through the realms of C# and C++, we aim to strike a delicate balance between theory and practice, providing you with clear explanations, practical examples, and thought-provoking projects. We understand that programming is not merely a technical pursuit but an art form that demands creativity, problem-solving skills, and an understanding of real-world applications. With each chapter, we empower you to develop your coding prowess, bridging the gap between theoretical concepts and tangible achievements.

We invite you to join us on this expedition through the realms of C# and C++, where you will acquire the knowledge, skills, and confidence to create exceptional applications, tackle complex challenges, and shape a successful career. Let this book be your compass as you navigate the intricacies of these languages, unlocking the boundless potential that awaits you in the world of programming.

So, without further ado, let us embark on this remarkable journey and discover the captivating landscapes of C# and C++ together.

Book 1 - C# Programming: The Essential Guide for Beginners

ANDREW SULLIVAN

Introduction: Getting Started

In recent years, the field of programming has experienced significant growth and has become an integral part of various industries. Among the many programming languages available, C# (pronounced "C sharp") has emerged as a powerful and versatile language for developing a wide range of applications. Whether you are a complete beginner or have some experience with programming, this guide aims to provide you with the essential knowledge and skills needed to start your journey into C# programming.

As with any new endeavor, it is crucial to have a solid understanding of the fundamentals. In the realm of programming, this means grasping the basic concepts and syntax of the language. C# is an object-oriented programming language developed by Microsoft, and it is widely used for building applications on the .NET platform. It offers a combination of simplicity, flexibility, and performance, making it an excellent choice for both beginners and experienced developers.

Before diving into the intricacies of C# programming, it is important to have the necessary tools in place. You will need a text editor or an integrated development environment (IDE) to write and compile your code. Popular choices for C# development include Visual Studio, Visual Studio Code, and JetBrains Rider. These tools provide a rich set of features and an intuitive interface to enhance your coding experience.

Once you have the necessary tools, the next step is to familiarize yourself with the basic structure of a C# program. A C# program typically consists of classes, methods, and statements. Classes serve as blueprints for creating objects, which are instances of those classes. Methods are blocks of code that perform specific tasks, and statements are individual instructions within those methods.

Understanding data types is fundamental in any programming language. C# offers various built-in data types, such as integers, floating-point numbers, characters, booleans, and strings, which allow you to store and manipulate different kinds of information. It is important to know how to declare variables of these types, assign values to them, and perform operations on them.

Control structures play a vital role in controlling the flow of execution in a program. C# provides several control structures, including conditionals (such as if-else statements and switch statements) and loops (such as for loops and while loops). These structures enable you to make decisions and repeat actions based on specific conditions, enhancing the flexibility and functionality of your programs.

Modularity and reusability are key principles in programming. C# supports the concept of classes and objects, allowing you to organize your code into reusable components. You can create your own classes and define their properties and behaviors, which can then be instantiated as objects and utilized throughout your program. This promotes code reusability, improves maintainability, and simplifies the overall development process.

Additionally, C# provides powerful features like exception handling, which enables you to handle errors and exceptional situations gracefully, preventing your program from crashing. It also supports input and output operations, enabling interaction with the user through the console or graphical user interfaces.

As you progress in your C# programming journey, you will encounter more advanced topics, such as object-oriented programming concepts, file I/O operations, database connectivity, and graphical user interface development. These topics build upon the foundational knowledge covered in this guide and open up a world of possibilities for creating sophisticated and robust applications.

So, let's dive in and explore the world of C# programming together!

An Overview of C# and Its Place in the World of Programming

In the ever-evolving landscape of programming languages, C# has emerged as a prominent player, offering a powerful and versatile platform for developing a wide range of applications. Developed by Microsoft, C# is an object-oriented programming language that has gained popularity among developers for its simplicity, flexibility, and performance.

C# was introduced in the early 2000s as part of Microsoft's .NET initiative, a framework that provides tools and resources for building applications across various platforms. Since its inception, C# has garnered a strong following and has become a widely adopted language in industries such as web development, game development, desktop applications, and mobile app development.

One of the key features that sets C# apart from other programming languages is its focus on object-oriented programming (OOP). In OOP, code is organized into objects that represent real-world entities, and these objects interact with each other to accomplish specific tasks. This paradigm allows for modular and reusable code, making it easier to manage and maintain large-scale projects.

C# offers a rich set of features that facilitate efficient and effective programming. It has a robust type system, providing built-in data types such as integers, floating-point numbers, characters, booleans, and strings, as well as the ability to define custom types through classes and structures. This versatility allows developers to handle a wide range of data and create complex data structures.

The language also supports a variety of control structures, including conditionals and loops, which enable developers to make decisions and repeat actions based on specific conditions. Additionally, C# provides comprehensive support for exception handling, allowing developers to catch and handle errors in a controlled manner, ensuring the stability and reliability of their applications.

C# is known for its seamless integration with the .NET platform. The .NET framework provides a vast collection of libraries and APIs (Application Programming Interfaces) that simplify common programming tasks. These libraries cover areas such as user interface development, database connectivity, networking, file I/O, and more, allowing developers to leverage existing functionality and focus on the core logic of their applications.

With the rise of cross-platform development, C# has expanded its reach beyond the Windows ecosystem. The introduction of .NET Core, a cross-platform version of the .NET framework, has enabled developers to build C# applications that run on Windows, macOS, and Linux. This versatility has opened up new possibilities for developers to create applications that can reach a wider audience across multiple platforms.

Furthermore, C# integrates well with other programming languages, making it suitable for interoperability and collaboration within a larger software ecosystem. It can interface with existing C and C++ codebases through platform invocation services, enabling developers to leverage legacy code or take advantage of performance-critical components written in other languages.

Installing the Necessary Tools to Start Writing C# Code

When embarking on your journey to learn C# programming, one of the first steps is to set up the necessary tools to write and compile your code. By installing the required software, you'll create an environment that enables you to write, test, and run your C# programs. In this section, we will guide you through the process of installing the essential tools to start writing C# code.

The primary tool you need is a text editor or an integrated development environment (IDE) that supports C# development. There are several popular options available, each with its own set of features and advantages. Let's explore a few of the most commonly used tools:

1. **Visual Studio:** Developed by Microsoft, Visual Studio is a powerful and comprehensive IDE for C# programming. It offers a wide range of features, including code editing, debugging, version control integration, and a rich set of built-in tools. Visual Studio provides a user-friendly interface and is available in different editions, such as Visual Studio Community (free), Visual Studio Professional, and Visual Studio Enterprise.

2. **Visual Studio Code:** Visual Studio Code, often referred to as VS Code, is a lightweight and versatile code editor. It is highly customizable and supports C# development through the use of extensions. VS Code offers features like syntax highlighting, code completion, debugging, and Git integration. It is free and available for Windows, macOS, and Linux.

3. **JetBrains Rider:** JetBrains Rider is a cross-platform IDE specifically designed for .NET and C# development. It provides a comprehensive set of features, including intelligent code completion, refactoring tools, debugging capabilities, and integration with version control systems. JetBrains Rider offers a free trial, and different licensing options are available for personal and commercial use.

Once you have chosen the appropriate tool for your needs, you can proceed with the installation process. Most IDEs provide straightforward installation wizards that guide you through the setup steps. Here's a general outline of the installation process:

1. Download the installer: Visit the official website of the chosen tool and locate the download page. Choose the appropriate version for your operating system and initiate the download.

2. Run the installer: Once the download is complete, run the installer file to start the installation process. Follow the on-screen instructions and select any additional features or settings you want to include during installation.

3. Configure the installation: Some IDEs may prompt you to customize certain installation settings, such as the installation location or additional components. Review and adjust these settings according to your preferences.

4. Complete the installation: After configuring the installation options, proceed with the installation process. The installer will copy the necessary files and set up the IDE on your system. This may take a few minutes, depending on your system's performance.

5. Launch the IDE: Once the installation is complete, you can launch the IDE from the Start menu or desktop shortcut. The IDE will open with a welcome screen or an empty project, ready for you to start coding.

It's worth noting that some IDEs may require additional dependencies, such as the .NET Framework or the .NET Core SDK. These dependencies are usually included in the installation process or can be downloaded separately if needed.

Installing the necessary tools to start writing C# code is a crucial step for beginners. By choosing a suitable IDE and following the installation instructions provided, you can create an environment that supports C# development. Whether you opt for Visual Studio, Visual Studio Code, JetBrains Rider, or any other C# IDE, having the right tools in place will empower you to explore the world of C# programming and unleash your creativity.

Chapter 1: Introduction to C# Programming

In the ever-evolving world of programming, learning a new language can be both exciting and daunting. For beginners, taking the first steps into the world of coding can feel like entering uncharted territory. However, with the right guidance and a solid understanding of the fundamentals, learning a programming language like C# can be a rewarding and fulfilling experience. This chapter serves as an introduction to C# programming, providing beginners with a solid foundation to build upon.

C# is an object-oriented programming language that was introduced in the early 2000s as part of the .NET initiative and has since become one of the most popular languages for building a wide range of applications. C# is known for its simplicity, flexibility, and performance, making it an excellent choice for both beginners and experienced programmers.

At its core, C# is designed to be a general-purpose language that can be used for various types of application development. Whether you want to build desktop applications, web applications, mobile apps, or even games, C# provides the tools and features necessary to bring your ideas to life.

One of the key concepts in C# programming is object-oriented programming (OOP). OOP is a programming paradigm that focuses on organizing code into reusable objects that represent real-world entities. These objects have properties (attributes) and behaviors (methods), and they interact with each other to perform specific tasks. This approach promotes code reusability, modularity, and maintainability, allowing developers to create complex applications with ease.

C# also offers a rich set of features that enable developers to write efficient and readable code. Some of these features include:

1. Strong typing: C# is a statically typed language, which means that variables must be declared with their respective types. This ensures type safety and helps catch errors at compile-time.

2. Automatic memory management: C# utilizes a garbage collector to automatically manage memory allocation and deallocation. This feature relieves developers from the

burden of manual memory management, making the language more accessible to beginners.

3. Exception handling: C# provides robust support for handling exceptions, which are runtime errors that can occur during program execution. With exception handling, developers can gracefully handle and recover from errors, preventing their programs from crashing.

4. Extensive standard library: C# comes with a comprehensive standard library that provides a wide range of pre-built classes and functions. This library offers functionalities for tasks such as file I/O, networking, data manipulation, and user interface development, saving developers time and effort in implementing common functionalities.

To start writing C# code, you will need an integrated development environment (IDE) or a text editor with C# support. Popular choices include Visual Studio, Visual Studio Code, and JetBrains Rider, as mentioned earlier. These tools provide a user-friendly interface, syntax highlighting, code completion, and debugging capabilities, among other helpful features.

As a beginner, it's important to familiarize yourself with the basic structure of a C# program. A typical C# program consists of classes, methods, and statements. Classes act as blueprints for creating objects, methods define the behavior of those objects, and statements are individual instructions within those methods.

Throughout this guide, we will explore various concepts, including data types, variables, control structures, and object-oriented programming principles, in more detail. By mastering these foundational concepts, you will gain the skills necessary to write C# code and develop your own applications.

Understanding the fundamentals of C# and its object-oriented nature sets the stage for your journey into the world of coding. With the right tools and a solid understanding of the core concepts, you are well on your way to becoming a proficient C# programmer.

Brief History of C# and Its Uses

In the dynamic world of programming languages, C# holds a significant place as a versatile and powerful language for software development. Understanding the history and context of C# can provide valuable insights into its evolution and practical applications. In this chapter, we will explore the brief history of C# and delve into its various uses in the world of programming.

C# was first introduced by Microsoft in the early 2000s as part of its .NET initiative. The primary goal behind the creation of C# was to develop a modern, object-oriented programming language that would seamlessly integrate with the .NET platform. It was designed to be simple, efficient, and capable of building a wide range of applications, from desktop software to web applications and mobile apps.

The development of C# was heavily influenced by other programming languages, particularly C, C++, and Java. By incorporating the best features of these languages, C# aimed to provide developers with a familiar and intuitive programming experience. The syntax of C# bears similarities to C and C++, making it easier for programmers who are already familiar with those languages to transition to C#.

One of the significant milestones in the history of C# was the release of the .NET Framework in 2002, which provided the runtime environment and a comprehensive set of libraries for developing and executing C# applications. This framework enabled developers to build robust and scalable applications with ease, leveraging the extensive collection of pre-built components and functionality.

Over the years, C# has evolved and matured, with Microsoft releasing several versions and updates to the language. Each new release brought improvements, new features, and increased performance. Notable versions of C# include C# 2.0, C# 3.0, C# 4.0, C# 5.0, C# 6.0, C# 7.0, C# 8.0, and C# 9.0. These updates introduced enhancements such as generics, LINQ (Language Integrated Query), asynchronous programming, pattern matching, and more.

The field of software development has witnessed the extensive use of C# across various domains. C# is widely utilized for building desktop applications using frameworks like Windows Presentation Foundation (WPF) and Windows Forms. It provides a rich set of tools and libraries that facilitate the creation of visually appealing and feature-rich applications for the Windows operating system.

C# has also gained popularity in web development, primarily through the use of ASP.NET, a web application framework. With ASP.NET, developers can build dynamic and interactive web applications, including websites, web services, and APIs. The framework offers seamless integration with databases, robust security features, and scalability.

Moreover, C# is a prominent language in the world of game development. The Unity game engine, which is widely used for creating games across multiple platforms, employs C# as its primary scripting language. By leveraging the power of C# in Unity, developers can build immersive and engaging gaming experiences.

In addition to these domains, C# is utilized in areas such as mobile app development, Internet of Things (IoT), cloud computing, data analysis, and more. Its versatility, performance, and wide range of frameworks and libraries make it a preferred choice for developers working on diverse projects.

Basic Structure of a C# Program

In the realm of programming languages, C# stands tall as a versatile and powerful tool for developers. With its intuitive syntax, extensive libraries, and broad range of applications, C# has garnered a significant following, making it an ideal choice for beginners seeking to embark on their coding journey.

Structure of a C# Program

At its core, a C# program is composed of classes, which serve as blueprints defining the structure and behavior of objects. Each class contains a set of variables, methods, and properties that encapsulate data and functionality within a specific context.

To comprehend the structure of a C# program, let's examine a simple example:

using System;

```
namespace MyFirstCSharpProgram
{
    class Program
    {
        static void Main(string[] args)
        {
            Console.WriteLine("Hello, world!");
        }
    }
}
```

In this example, we begin with the **using** directive, which allows us to include external libraries or namespaces that provide additional functionality. In this case, we include the **System** namespace, which provides access to the fundamental types and basic functionality of the .NET Framework.

Next, we encounter the **namespace** declaration. A namespace serves as a container for related classes and helps organize code, preventing naming conflicts. In our example, we define a namespace named **MyFirstCSharpProgram**.

Within the namespace, we define a class called **Program**. This class represents the entry point of our program. The **Program** class contains a single method called **Main**, which serves as the starting point for program execution. The **Main** method is declared with the **static** modifier, indicating that it belongs to the class itself rather than an instance of the class.

The **Main** method takes a parameter of type **string[]**, commonly referred to as **args**. This parameter allows us to pass command-line arguments to the program.

Inside the **Main** method, we have a single line of code: **Console.WriteLine("Hello, world!");**. This line utilizes the **Console.WriteLine** method to output the message "Hello, world!" to the console. The **Console** class belongs to the **System** namespace and provides a range of methods for interacting with the console window.

The Role of the Main Method

The **Main** method serves as the entry point for our C# program. When we execute a C# application, the runtime environment looks for the **Main** method to begin program execution. The **Main** method is where the flow of control starts and where we typically initialize our application and define the primary logic.

By convention, the **Main** method must be declared with the following signature:

static void Main(string[] args)

Here, the **static** keyword indicates that the **Main** method can be invoked without creating an instance of the class. The **void** keyword specifies that the **Main** method does not return a value. The parameter **string[] args** allows us to access any command-line arguments passed to the program.

It is important to note that a C# program can have only one **Main** method, acting as the single entry point for the application. However, multiple classes can exist within a program, each with its own unique set of methods and functionality.

Building and Executing a C# Program

To transform our C# code into a runnable application, we need to compile it into an executable file. The C# compiler takes our human-readable code and translates it into instructions that the computer can understand and execute.

Once we compile our code, we can execute the resulting executable file, launching our C# program. The program starts executing from the **Main** method, and the instructions within the method dictate the program's behavior.

Executing a C# program can be done through various means, including using an Integrated Development Environment (IDE) such as Visual Studio, or through command-line tools like the .NET Core command-line interface (CLI). These tools provide a convenient way to compile and run our C# programs, providing a seamless development experience.

Chapter 2: C# Basics: Variables, Data Types, Operators

As we delve deeper into the world of C# programming, it is crucial to establish a strong foundation in the fundamental building blocks of the language. In this chapter, we explore the essential concepts of variables, data types, and operators in C#. Understanding these concepts is vital as they form the bedrock of any C# program, allowing us to manipulate and process data effectively.

Variables: Storing and Manipulating Data

In programming, a variable serves as a container for storing and manipulating data. It is a named memory location that can hold a value of a specific data type. Variables allow us to work with data dynamically, enabling us to perform calculations, store user inputs, and keep track of information within our programs.

To declare a variable in C#, we follow a specific syntax:

dataType variableName;

Here, **dataType** represents the type of data the variable can hold, and **variableName** is the name we assign to the variable. For example, let's declare a variable of type **int** (integer):

int myNumber;

In this example, we declare a variable named **myNumber** of type **int**. The **int** data type represents whole numbers without decimal points.

To assign a value to a variable, we use the assignment operator (**=**):

myNumber = 42;

Now, the variable **myNumber** holds the value **42**.

We can also declare and assign a value to a variable in a single line:

int myNumber = 42;

It is important to note that variable names in C# are case-sensitive, meaning **myNumber** and **mynumber** would be treated as two distinct variables.

Data Types: Categorizing Data in C#

C# provides various data types to accommodate different kinds of data. Each data type has specific characteristics and memory requirements. Understanding the appropriate data type for each piece of data is crucial for efficient memory usage and ensuring accurate data manipulation.

Some commonly used data types in C# include:

- **int**: Represents integers (whole numbers) without decimal points.
- **float** and **double**: Represent real numbers with decimal points, with **double** providing higher precision.
- **char**: Represents a single character.
- **string**: Represents a sequence of characters.
- **bool**: Represents a boolean value (**true** or **false**).
- **DateTime**: Represents a date and time value.

These are just a few examples of the many data types available in C#. Choosing the appropriate data type for a variable depends on the nature of the data it will hold and the desired precision or range.

Operators: Performing Operations on Data

Operators in C# enable us to perform various operations on data, such as arithmetic calculations, logical evaluations, and comparisons. They allow us to manipulate and combine variables and values to produce desired outcomes.

C# supports a wide range of operators, including:

- Arithmetic operators: **+** (addition), **-** (subtraction), ***** (multiplication), **/** (division), **%** (modulus), etc.
- Assignment operators: **=** (assignment), **+=** (addition assignment), **-=**, ***=**, **/=**, etc.
- Comparison operators: **==** (equality), **!=** (inequality), **>**, **<**, **>=**, **<=**, etc.
- Logical operators: **&&** (logical AND), **||** (logical OR), **!** (logical NOT), etc.
- Increment and decrement operators: **++** (increment by 1), **--** (decrement by 1).

These operators allow us to manipulate variables and perform calculations, make decisions based on conditions, and control the flow of our programs.

For example, let's consider the following code snippet:

```
int x = 5;
int y = 3;
int sum = x + y;
```

In this example, we declare two variables **x** and **y**, assigning them the values **5** and **3**, respectively. We then use the addition operator (**+**) to calculate the sum of **x** and **y** and store the result in the variable **sum**. After execution, **sum** will hold the value **8**.

It is worth noting that different data types may have specific operators designed for their characteristics. For example, the **+** operator performs addition for numeric types, but it concatenates strings when used with string data types

Understanding the Various Types of Variables and Data Types in C#

In the world of programming, variables play a crucial role in storing and manipulating data. They allow us to work with different types of information and perform calculations, comparisons, and other operations.

Variables: Containers for Data

Variables in C# serve as containers that hold values of different types. They enable us to store and access data throughout our programs, making it possible to perform computations, store user inputs, and track information dynamically. Before we can utilize variables, it is important to understand the different types available in C#.

Data Types in C#

C# provides a rich set of data types, each designed to handle specific kinds of data. By choosing the appropriate data type for a variable, we can ensure efficient memory usage and accurate representation of our data. Let's explore some of the commonly used data types in C#:

- **int**: The **int** data type represents integer values, which are whole numbers without decimal points. For example, **5**, **-10**, and **0** are all integers.

- **double** and **float**: These data types are used to represent real numbers with decimal points. The **double** type offers higher precision compared to the **float** type. For instance, **3.14** and **2.71828** are examples of real numbers.

- **char**: The **char** data type represents single characters, such as letters, digits, or symbols. It is enclosed in single quotes, like **'A'**, **'5'**, or **'%'**.

- **string**: The **string** data type represents sequences of characters. It is used to store text or multiple characters. For example, **"Hello, world!"** or **"OpenAI"** are string values.

- **bool**: The **bool** data type represents boolean values, which can be either **true** or **false**. Booleans are often used in logical operations and conditional statements.

- **DateTime**: The **DateTime** data type is used to represent date and time values. It provides functionality to manipulate dates, perform calculations, and format dates in various ways.

These are just a few examples of the data types available in C#. Each data type has its own characteristics, limitations, and appropriate use cases. Understanding the differences between data types is crucial to ensure that our variables hold the correct type of data and that operations are performed accurately.

Declaring Variables in C#

To use a variable in C#, we need to declare it, specifying its data type and assigning an initial value if necessary. The syntax for declaring a variable is as follows:

dataType variableName;

Here, **dataType** represents the desired data type of the variable, and **variableName** is the name we assign to it. For example, to declare an integer variable called **age**, we would use the following declaration:

int age;

In this case, we declare a variable named **age** of type **int**, ready to store integer values.

We can also assign an initial value to a variable during declaration:

int count = 0;

In this example, we declare a variable named **count** and assign it an initial value of **0**.

Variables can be declared and assigned values later in the code, or their values can be modified during program execution using assignment statements.

Type Inference in C#

In C#, there is a feature called type inference that allows the compiler to automatically determine the data type of a variable based on its initial value. This eliminates the need to explicitly specify the data type during declaration. For example:

var name = "John";

In this case, the compiler infers that the variable **name** is of type **string** because it is initialized with a string value.

It is important to note that although type inference can be convenient, it is still recommended to explicitly specify the data type when it enhances code readability or when the variable's type might not be immediately evident.

Understanding Variable Naming Conventions

When naming variables in C#, it is important to follow certain naming conventions to improve code readability and maintainability. Here are some common conventions:

- Variable names should be descriptive, reflecting the purpose and content of the data they hold. For example, **age**, **userName**, or **totalPrice** are meaningful names.

- Variable names should start with a lowercase letter and use camel casing, where each subsequent word starts with an uppercase letter. For example, **studentName** or **numberOfApples**.

- Avoid using reserved keywords as variable names, as they have special meanings in the C# language.

By following these conventions, we can make our code more understandable, helping ourselves and other developers who may read or maintain our code in the future.

Basic Operations in C#

In C# programming, basic operations involve manipulating and performing calculations on variables and data. These operations allow us to process data, perform mathematical computations, and make decisions based on conditions. In this section, we will explore some of the essential basic operations available in C#.

Arithmetic Operations

Arithmetic operations in C# involve performing mathematical calculations on numeric values. C# provides a set of operators for addition (+), subtraction (-), multiplication (*), division (/), and modulus (%). These operators enable us to perform calculations and manipulate numeric data.

For example, consider the following code snippet:

```
int x = 5;
int y = 3;
int sum = x + y;        // Addition
int difference = x - y;    // Subtraction
int product = x * y;   // Multiplication
int quotient = x / y;  // Division
int remainder = x % y; // Modulus
```

In this example, we declare two variables **x** and **y** with values of **5** and **3**, respectively. We then use the arithmetic operators to perform addition, subtraction, multiplication, division, and modulus operations. The results are stored in separate variables (**sum**, **difference**, **product**, **quotient**, and **remainder**).

Assignment Operators

Assignment operators are used to assign values to variables. The most common assignment operator is the equals sign (=). It assigns the value on the right-hand side to the variable on the left-hand side.

For example:

```
int num1 = 10;
int num2 = 5;


num1 += num2;  // Equivalent to num1 = num1 + num2;
```

In this example, the **+=** assignment operator is used to add **num2** to **num1** and assign the result back to **num1**. The final value of **num1** becomes **15**.

Other assignment operators include **-=** (subtract and assign), ***=** (multiply and assign), **/=** (divide and assign), and **%=** (modulus and assign).

Comparison Operators

Comparison operators in C# are used to compare values and evaluate conditions. These operators return a Boolean value (**true** or **false**) based on the comparison result. Common comparison operators include **==** (equality), **!=** (inequality), **>** (greater than), **<** (less than), **>=** (greater than or equal to), and **<=** (less than or equal to).

For example:

int a = 5;

int b = 7;

bool isEqual = (a == b);   // false

bool isGreaterThan = (a > b);   // false

bool isLessThan = (a < b);   // true

In this example, we compare the values of **a** and **b** using the equality (**==**), greater than (**>**), and less than (**<**) operators. The results are stored in Boolean variables (**isEqual, isGreaterThan, and isLessThan**).

Logical Operators

Logical operators in C# are used to combine or evaluate logical conditions. The three main logical operators are **&&** (logical AND), **||** (logical OR), and **!** (logical NOT).

For example:

bool isTrue = true;

bool isFalse = false;

bool result1 = (isTrue && isFalse); // false

bool result2 = (isTrue || isFalse); // true

bool result3 = !isTrue;   // false

In this example, we use logical operators to combine or negate Boolean values (**isTrue** and **isFalse**). The results are stored in separate Boolean variables (**result1**, **result2**, and **result3**).

String Concatenation

In C#, we can concatenate strings using the **+** operator. String concatenation allows us to combine multiple strings into a single string.

For example:

string greeting = "Hello";

string name = "John";

string message = greeting + " " + name;   // "Hello John"

In this example, we concatenate the strings **greeting**, a space, and **name** to form the final string stored in the **message** variable.

Chapter 3: Decision-Making and Loops in C#

Conditional Statements and Loops in C#

In the world of programming, decision-making and repetition are fundamental concepts that allow us to control the flow of our programs and make them more dynamic. In C#, conditional statements and loops provide the necessary tools to incorporate decision-making and repetition into our code.

Conditional Statements

Conditional statements in C# enable us to make decisions and execute different blocks of code based on specific conditions. They allow our programs to adapt and respond dynamically to different scenarios. The most commonly used conditional statements in C# are the **if**, **if-else**, and **switch** statements.

The if Statement

The **if** statement is the simplest form of conditional statement. It allows us to execute a block of code only if a specific condition is true. The syntax for the **if** statement is as follows:

```
if (condition)
{
    // Code to execute if the condition is true
}
```

For example:

```
int x = 5;

if (x > 0)
{
```

```
Console.WriteLine("x is positive");
}
```

In this example, if the value of **x** is greater than 0, the message "x is positive" will be displayed. Otherwise, if the condition is false, the code block inside the **if** statement will be skipped.

The if-else Statement

The **if-else** statement allows us to execute different blocks of code based on the evaluation of a condition. If the condition is true, the code inside the **if** block is executed. If the condition is false, the code inside the **else** block is executed. The syntax for the **if-else** statement is as follows:

```
if (condition)
{
    // Code to execute if the condition is true
}
else
{
    // Code to execute if the condition is false
}
```

For example:

```
int x = 5;


if (x > 0)
{
    Console.WriteLine("x is positive");
}
else
{
    Console.WriteLine("x is not positive");
}
```

In this example, if the value of **x** is greater than 0, the message "x is positive" will be displayed. Otherwise, if the condition is false, the message "x is not positive" will be displayed.

The switch Statement

The **switch** statement provides a way to evaluate multiple conditions and execute different blocks of code based on the value of a variable. It offers a more concise alternative to multiple **if-else** statements when there are many possible conditions. The syntax for the **switch** statement is as follows:

```
switch (variable)
{
    case value1:
        // Code to execute if variable equals value1
        break;
    case value2:
        // Code to execute if variable equals value2
        break;
    // Add more cases as needed
    default:
        // Code to execute if none of the cases match
        break;
}
```

For example:

```
int dayOfWeek = 3;

switch (dayOfWeek)
{
    case 1:
        Console.WriteLine("Monday");
        break;
    case 2:
        Console.WriteLine("Tuesday");
        break;
```

```
case 3:
    Console.WriteLine("Wednesday");
    break;
default:
    Console.WriteLine("Other day");
    break;
}
```

In this example, the value of **dayOfWeek** is 3, so the message "Wednesday" will be displayed.

Loops

Loops in C# allow us to repeat blocks of code multiple times, making our programs more efficient and flexible. They are invaluable when we need to iterate over collections, perform repetitive calculations, or carry out other tasks that require repetition. The most commonly used loops in C# are the **for**, **while**, and **do-while** loops.

The for Loop

The **for** loop is used when we know the number of iterations in advance. It consists of three parts: initialization, condition, and iteration.

The while Loop

The **while** loop is used when we want to repeat a block of code as long as a certain condition is true. The condition is evaluated before each iteration.

The do-while Loop

The **do-while** loop is similar to the **while** loop, but the condition is evaluated after each iteration. This guarantees that the loop body is executed at least once.

Understanding Flow Control in C# Programs

Flow control plays a crucial role in C# programming as it determines the sequence in which statements and instructions are executed. By utilizing flow control constructs effectively, we can control the execution path of our programs, making them more dynamic and responsive.

Conditional Statements

Conditional statements are fundamental to flow control in C#. They allow us to make decisions and execute different code blocks based on specific conditions. In addition to the conditional statements mentioned earlier, let's explore some additional aspects:

Ternary Operator

The ternary operator, **? :**, is a concise way to write conditional statements in a single line. It allows us to assign values based on a condition. The syntax is as follows:

variable = (condition) ? value1 : value2;

If the condition is true, **value1** is assigned to the variable; otherwise, **value2** is assigned. Here's an example:

int age = 20;

string message = (age >= 18) ? "You are an adult" : "You are a minor";

In this example, if **age** is greater than or equal to 18, the message "You are an adult" is assigned to the **message** variable. Otherwise, the message "You are a minor" is assigned.

Nested Conditional Statements

Nested conditional statements involve placing conditional statements within other conditional statements. This allows for more complex decision-making logic. For instance:

int score = 85;

if (score >= 90)

{

   Console. WriteLine("Excellent!");

}

else if (score >= 80)

{

   Console. WriteLine("Very Good!");

}

else if (score >= 70)

{

```
    Console.WriteLine("Good!");
}
else
{
    Console.WriteLine("Needs Improvement!");
}
```

In this example, the program evaluates the value of **score** and prints a corresponding message based on the condition that is met.

Looping Structures

Loops in C# enable the repetition of code blocks as long as certain conditions are met. They are useful when we need to perform a set of instructions repeatedly. Let's explore the common loop structures in C#:

The for Loop

The **for** loop allows us to repeat a block of code for a specified number of times. It consists of three parts: initialization, condition, and increment/decrement. Here's the basic syntax:

```
for (initialization; condition; increment/decrement)
{
    // Code block to repeat
}
```

For example:

```
for (int i = 1; i <= 5; i++)
{
    Console.WriteLine(i);
}
```

In this example, the loop iterates from **1** to **5**, printing the values of **i** on each iteration.

The while Loop

The **while** loop repeats a block of code as long as a specified condition remains true. It evaluates the condition before each iteration. The syntax is as follows:

```
while (condition)
```

```
{
    // Code block to repeat
}
```

For example:

```
int count = 0;
while (count < 5)
{
    Console.WriteLine(count);
    count++;
}
```

In this example, the loop repeats the code block as long as **count** is less than **5**. The value of **count** is incremented on each iteration.

The do-while Loop

The **do-while** loop is similar to the **while** loop, but it evaluates the condition after executing the code block. This ensures that the code block is executed at least once, regardless of the initial condition. Here's the syntax:

```
do
{
    // Code block to repeat
} while (condition);
```

For example:

```
int i = 0;
do
{
    Console.WriteLine(i);
    i++;
} while (i < 5);
```

In this example, the loop executes the code block and prints the value of **i** at least once. It continues to repeat the block as long as **i** is less than **5**.

The foreach Loop

The **foreach** loop simplifies the iteration over elements of an array or a collection. It automatically iterates through each element without the need for explicit indexing. Here's the syntax:

```
foreach (datatype variable in collection)
{
    // Code block to repeat
}
```

For example:

```
int[] numbers = { 1, 2, 3, 4, 5 };
foreach (int number in numbers)
{
    Console.WriteLine(number);
}
```

In this example, the loop iterates over each element in the **numbers** array and prints its value.

Chapter 4: Introduction to Object-Oriented Programming in C#

Defining and Using Classes in C#

Object-oriented programming (OOP) is a paradigm that allows us to structure our code in a way that models real-world objects and their interactions. In C#, classes are the building blocks of object-oriented programming. In this chapter, we will explore the concept of classes in C# and learn how to define and use them effectively.

Understanding Classes

In C#, a class is a blueprint or a template for creating objects. It defines the structure and behavior of an object by encapsulating data and methods. The data, also known as attributes or fields, represents the state of the object, while the methods define its behavior or functionality.

A class provides a way to organize related data and methods into a single unit. It promotes code reusability and allows for better maintenance and extensibility of code. By creating objects from classes, we can instantiate multiple instances with their own unique state and behavior.

Defining a Class

To define a class in C#, we use the **class** keyword followed by the class name. Let's take a look at a simple example of defining a class:

```
public class Person
{
    // Attributes
    public string Name;
    public int Age;
```

```
// Methods
public void SayHello()
{
    Console.WriteLine("Hello, my name is " + Name + " and I am " + Age + " years old.");
}
}
```

In this example, we define a class called **Person**. It has two attributes: **Name** of type **string** and **Age** of type **int**. We also have a method called **SayHello()** that prints a greeting message using the person's name and age.

Creating Objects from a Class

Once we have defined a class, we can create objects or instances of that class. Objects represent specific instances of the class and have their own unique state and behavior. To create an object, we use the **new** keyword followed by the class name and parentheses.

```
Person person1 = new Person();
```

In this example, we create an object **person1** of type **Person** using the **new** keyword. This object will have its own set of attributes and methods defined in the **Person** class.

Accessing Class Members

After creating an object from a class, we can access its attributes and methods using the dot notation (**.**). Let's see how we can access the attributes and methods of the **Person** class:

```
person1.Name = "John";
person1.Age = 25;
person1.SayHello();
```

In this code snippet, we assign values to the **Name** and **Age** attributes of the **person1** object. We then call the **SayHello()** method of the **person1** object, which prints a greeting message using the assigned values.

Encapsulation and Access Modifiers

Encapsulation is an important principle in OOP that ensures the proper access and visibility of class members. In C#, we can use access modifiers to control the accessibility of attributes and methods within a class.

The three common access modifiers in C# are:

- **public**: The public access modifier allows the attributes and methods to be accessed from anywhere, including outside the class.

- **private**: The private access modifier restricts the attributes and methods to be accessed only within the class itself.

- **protected**: The protected access modifier allows access to the attributes and methods within the class and its derived classes.

By default, if no access modifier is specified, the members are considered **private**.

Constructors

Constructors are special methods used to initialize objects of a class. They have the same name as the class and are invoked when creating a new object. Constructors enable us to set the initial state *of an object.*

Let's add a constructor to our **Person** class:

```
public class Person
{
    // Attributes
    public string Name;
    public int Age;

    // Constructor
    public Person(string name, int age)
    {
        Name = name;
        Age = age;
    }

    // Methods
    public void SayHello()
    {
```

```
Console.WriteLine("Hello, my name is " + Name + " and I am " + Age + " years old.");
   }
}
```

In this updated example, we added a constructor that takes parameters **name** and **age** and assigns them to the corresponding attributes.

Now, when creating a **Person** object, we can pass the values for **name** and **age** directly:

```
Person person2 = new Person("Alice", 30);

person2.SayHello();
```

By using constructors, we can ensure that the object is initialized properly with the required information.

Understanding Information Hiding and Visibility Management in C#

In object-oriented programming (OOP), one of the key principles is information hiding, also known as encapsulation. It refers to the practice of hiding the internal details of a class and exposing only the necessary information to the outside world. In C#, information hiding is achieved through visibility modifiers that control the accessibility of class members.

Visibility Modifiers

C# provides several visibility modifiers that allow us to control the accessibility of class members. The three common modifiers are:

- **public**: The public modifier makes the member accessible from anywhere, both within and outside the class. Public members are part of the class's public interface and can be accessed by other classes.

- **private**: The private modifier restricts the member's access to only within the same class. Private members are not visible to other classes or code outside the class. They are used to encapsulate the internal implementation details of a class.

- **protected**: The protected modifier allows access to the member within the class itself and its derived classes. Protected members are primarily used for inheritance scenarios, where derived classes need access to certain members of the base class.

By default, if no visibility modifier is specified, members are considered private.

Encapsulation and Information Hiding

Encapsulation is a fundamental concept in OOP that encompasses information hiding. It involves bundling the data and methods that operate on that data into a single unit, known as a class. The internal details of the class, such as the implementation and data representation, are hidden from other classes or external code. This promotes modularity, reusability, and code maintenance.

By hiding the internal implementation details, we protect the integrity of the class and prevent unauthorized access or modification of its data. This encapsulation allows for better control over the behavior and state of objects, leading to more robust and maintainable code.

Getters and Setters (Properties)

In C#, we commonly use getters and setters to provide controlled access to class attributes or fields. Getters allow us to retrieve the value of an attribute, while setters enable us to modify or update its value. By encapsulating attribute access through properties, we can enforce additional logic or constraints, such as data validation or calculations.

Let's consider an example:

```
public class Person
{
    private string name;
    public string Name
    {
        get { return name; }
        set { name = value; }
    }
}
```

In this example, we have a private field **name** and a corresponding public property **Name**. The getter (**get**) retrieves the value of **name**, and the setter (**set**) assigns a new value to it. By using properties, we can control how the name is accessed and updated, providing an additional layer of abstraction and encapsulation.

Benefits of Information Hiding

Information hiding offers several benefits in C# programming:

- Modularity: By hiding the internal implementation details, we can modify the class's implementation without affecting other parts of the code that use the class. This promotes modularity and code maintenance.

- Security: Hiding the internal details of a class prevents unauthorized access or modification of its data. It enhances the security of the application by limiting access to critical information.

- Code Reusability: Encapsulated classes with well-defined interfaces can be easily reused in different parts of an application or in other applications altogether. This promotes code reusability and reduces development time.

- Maintenance and Debugging: Encapsulation simplifies the maintenance and debugging process by localizing changes within a class. It isolates potential issues and allows for easier troubleshooting.

Best Practices

To effectively manage visibility and information hiding in your C# programs, consider the following best practices:

- Keep class members private by default: By default, mark class members as private unless there is a specific need for them to be accessible from outside the class. This ensures that the internal implementation remains hidden.

- Use properties instead of exposing fields directly: Properties provide a level of abstraction and allow for additional logic or validation in attribute access. They offer more control and flexibility when modifying the behavior of class attributes.

- Limit the exposure of internal details: Only expose the necessary information and functionality through the class's public interface. This helps maintain the integrity and clarity of the class.

- Document the intended use of class members: Clearly document the purpose and usage guidelines of class members to guide other developers who use or extend the class. This promotes proper usage and reduces potential misuse.

Chapter 5: Advanced Concepts in Object-Oriented Programming

Exploring Polymorphism

Polymorphism is a fundamental concept in object-oriented programming (OOP) that allows objects of different classes to be treated as objects of a common base class. It provides flexibility and extensibility in designing and implementing software systems. In this chapter, we will delve into polymorphism in C# and explore how it enables us to write more flexible and reusable code.

Understanding Polymorphism

Polymorphism is one of the four fundamental principles of Object-Oriented Programming (OOP), along with encapsulation, inheritance, and abstraction. The term "polymorphism" comes from the Greek words "poly" (many) and "morph" (form), and it refers to the ability of an object to take on many forms.

There are two types of polymorphism in OOP: compile-time polymorphism (also known as static polymorphism) and runtime polymorphism (also known as dynamic polymorphism).

Compile-Time Polymorphism (Static Polymorphism)

Compile-time polymorphism is achieved through method overloading and operator overloading.

- **Method Overloading**: This occurs when two or more methods in the same class have the same name but different parameters (either different number of parameters, or different types of parameters, or both). The correct method to call is determined at compile time based on the number and type of arguments.

- **Operator Overloading**: This is a specific case of polymorphism where different operators have different implementations depending on their arguments. Operator overloading is typically done to make user-defined types behave in the same way as built-in types.

Runtime Polymorphism (Dynamic Polymorphism)

Runtime polymorphism is achieved through method overriding and interfaces (in languages that support them, like Java and C#).

- **Method Overriding**: This occurs when a subclass provides a specific implementation of a method that is already provided by its parent class. The method in the subclass must have the same name, return type, and parameters as the one in the parent class. The version of the method to call (either the one in the parent class or the one in the subclass) is determined at runtime based on the type of the object.

- **Interfaces**: An interface is a contract that specifies a set of methods that a class must implement. Any class that implements an interface can be used wherever that interface is expected. This allows objects of different classes to be treated as objects of the same abstract type, leading to flexible and reusable code.

Polymorphism allows objects of different classes to be treated as objects of a common superclass or interface. This is particularly useful in large software systems where you want to reduce dependencies between components and make the system more modular and extensible. For example, you might have a piece of code that operates on a list of objects of type "Shape", which could be objects of any subclass of Shape, such as Circle, Square, or Triangle. Thanks to polymorphism, the code can work with any shape object, making it more flexible and reusable.

Inheritance and Polymorphism

Inheritance is a key feature of **OOP** that allows us to define a new class based on an existing class, known as the base class or superclass. The derived class inherits the attributes and methods of the base class and can also introduce its own unique attributes and methods.

Polymorphism takes advantage of inheritance by allowing us to create objects of the derived classes and use them interchangeably with objects of the base class. This is achieved through method overriding, where a derived class provides its own implementation of a method defined in the base class.

Method Overriding and Virtual Methods

Method overriding is the process of redefining a method in a derived class with the same signature as the method in the base class. By marking a method in the base class as **virtual** and overriding it in the derived class using the **override** keyword, we can provide specialized implementations of the method for each derived class.

Let's consider an example:

```
public class Shape
{
    public virtual void Draw()
    {
        Console.WriteLine("Drawing a shape");
    }
}


public class Circle : Shape
{
    public override void Draw()
    {
        Console.WriteLine("Drawing a circle");
    }
}


public class Square : Shape
{
    public override void Draw()
    {
        Console.WriteLine("Drawing a square");
    }
}
```

In this example, we have a base class **Shape** with a virtual method **Draw()**. The **Circle** and **Square** classes inherit from **Shape** and override the **Draw()** method with their own implementations.

Polymorphic Behavior

Using polymorphism, we can create objects of the derived classes and treat them as objects of the base class. This allows us to write code that operates on objects of different derived classes without the need for separate code blocks for each derived class.

Shape circle = new Circle();

Shape square = new Square();

circle.Draw(); // Output: "Drawing a circle"

square.Draw(); // Output: "Drawing a square"

In this code snippet, we create objects **circle** and **square** of type **Shape**, but they are actually instances of the **Circle** and **Square** classes, respectively. When we call the **Draw()** method on each object, the appropriate implementation defined in the derived class is executed.

This polymorphic behavior allows us to write more generic code that can handle different types of objects based on their shared base class, making our code more flexible and extensible.

Polymorphism with Abstract Classes and Interfaces

In addition to using inheritance and method overriding, polymorphism can also be achieved through abstract classes and interfaces. Abstract classes provide a partial implementation and serve as a base for derived classes, while interfaces define a contract that classes must adhere to.

Both abstract classes and interfaces allow us to achieve polymorphic behavior by defining a common set of methods or properties that derived classes must implement. This allows us to write code that can work with objects of different classes, as long as they adhere to the defined contract.

Digging Deeper into Class Definition, Encapsulation, and Visibility

In object-oriented programming (OOP), class definition, encapsulation, and visibility play crucial roles in designing robust and maintainable code. These concepts allow us to structure our programs effectively, encapsulate data and behavior within classes, and control the visibility of class members.

Class Definition

A class is a blueprint for creating objects in OOP. It defines a set of properties and methods that are common to all objects of one type.

In a class definition, you specify the data members (variables) and member functions (methods). The data members represent the state of an object, and the member functions represent the behavior of an object.

A class definition can also include constructors, which are special methods that are called when an object is created. Constructors often set the initial state of an object.

Inheritance is another important concept in class definition. A class can inherit properties and methods from another class. This allows for code reuse and is a way to model a "is-a" relationship. For example, a "Car" class might inherit from a more general "Vehicle" class.

Encapsulation

Encapsulation is one of the four fundamental principles of OOP (the others being inheritance, polymorphism, and abstraction). It refers to the bundling of data, and the methods that operate on that data, into a single unit called an object.

Encapsulation helps to achieve data hiding and security. It prevents the data from being accessed directly from outside the class. Instead, data can only be accessed or modified through the class's methods, which are often referred to as getters (for accessing data) and setters (for modifying data).

Encapsulation makes it possible to change the implementation of a class without affecting other parts of the program that use the class. This is because the implementation details are hidden behind the class's methods.

Visibility

Visibility refers to the accessibility of the data members and member functions from outside the class. There are three levels of visibility in most OOP languages:

- **Private**: The members declared as private can be accessed only within the same class. They are not visible to other classes.

- **Public**: The members declared as public can be accessed from any part of the program.

- **Protected**: The members declared as protected can be accessed within the same class and by the classes that are derived from that class.

The concept of visibility is closely related to encapsulation. By making data members private or protected, a class can hide its internal state and prevent it from being modified directly from outside the class. This helps to maintain the integrity of the object's state.

Chapter 6: Real-World C# Applications

Real-World Examples of C# Usage

C# is a versatile and powerful programming language that finds application in various real-world scenarios. In this chapter, we will explore some common domains and industries where C# is widely used, showcasing how this language can be leveraged to develop practical and impactful applications.

Web Development

C# is extensively utilized in web development, enabling developers to build dynamic and interactive web applications. Microsoft's ASP.NET framework provides a robust ecosystem for creating web applications using C#. With ASP.NET, developers can leverage the Model-View-Controller (MVC) architectural pattern to create scalable and maintainable web solutions. C# in conjunction with technologies like Razor Pages and Entity Framework allows for seamless integration with databases, enabling the development of data-driven web applications.

Real-world examples of C# usage in web development include:

- Content management systems (CMS): C# and ASP.NET can power feature-rich CMS platforms, allowing users to create, manage, and publish digital content easily.

- E-commerce websites: C# can be used to build secure and scalable e-commerce platforms, facilitating online transactions, inventory management, and customer interaction.

- Customer relationship management (CRM) systems: C# enables the development of CRM systems that assist organizations in managing customer interactions, sales processes, and data analysis.

Desktop Applications

C# provides a robust framework for developing desktop applications, allowing developers to create intuitive and feature-rich software for Windows-based systems. The Windows Presentation

Foundation (WPF) framework, along with C#, empowers developers to build visually appealing and interactive desktop applications with seamless data binding capabilities.

Real-world examples of C# usage in desktop applications include:

- Productivity tools: C# can be utilized to develop applications such as text editors, spreadsheet software, and project management tools, enhancing productivity and facilitating efficient workflows.

- Financial applications: C# enables the creation of desktop applications for financial institutions, including banking software, stock trading platforms, and accounting systems.

- Scientific and engineering tools: C# can be employed to build scientific analysis tools, data visualization software, and engineering simulations, aiding professionals in their research and analysis tasks.

Game Development

C# has gained popularity as a language for game development, thanks to its integration with the Unity game engine. Unity provides a powerful and user-friendly environment for creating games across multiple platforms, including desktop, mobile, and consoles. By utilizing C# scripting in Unity, developers can implement game mechanics, create interactive gameplay elements, and manage in-game behavior.

Real-world examples of C# usage in game development include:

- Mobile games: C# is extensively used in the development of mobile games for iOS and Android platforms. It allows developers to create engaging and visually stunning games optimized for mobile devices.

- Virtual reality (VR) and augmented reality (AR) experiences: C# and Unity enable the development of immersive VR and AR applications, allowing users to explore virtual worlds and interact with virtual objects.

Enterprise Software

C# is widely employed in the development of enterprise-level software solutions. It offers powerful frameworks and libraries that facilitate the creation of scalable, secure, and reliable applications tailored to the needs of businesses.

Real-world examples of C# usage in enterprise software include:

- Enterprise resource planning (ERP) systems: C# can be used to build comprehensive ERP systems that integrate and manage various business processes, such as finance, human resources, and supply chain management.

- Customer service and support applications: C# enables the development of applications that streamline customer support processes, including ticket management, knowledge bases, and live chat systems.

- Data analytics and business intelligence (BI) tools: C# can be utilized to create data analytics and BI applications that help organizations extract valuable insights from large datasets, facilitating informed decision-making.

Overview of Industries and Projects that Use C#

C# is a widely adopted programming language that finds extensive usage across various industries and projects. Its versatility, robustness, and integration capabilities make it a popular choice for developing a wide range of applications. In this chapter, we will explore some of the key industries and projects where C# is prominently utilized, highlighting the diverse applications and opportunities available for C# developers.

Software Development and Technology

C# is an integral part of the Microsoft technology stack and is widely used for software development within the Microsoft ecosystem. From desktop applications to web development and cloud-based solutions, C# plays a crucial role in building cutting-edge software products and services. Many software companies and technology-driven organizations leverage C# to create innovative and scalable solutions.

Real-world examples of C# usage in software development and technology include:

- Microsoft Office Suite: C# is employed in building add-ins, macros, and customizations for Microsoft Office applications such as Word, Excel, and Outlook.

- Enterprise software solutions: C# is utilized in the development of comprehensive enterprise software systems, including customer relationship management (CRM), enterprise resource planning (ERP), and supply chain management (SCM) solutions.

- Cloud computing: C# is integrated with Microsoft Azure, allowing developers to build cloud-based applications, scalable web services, and serverless functions.

Web and Application Development

C# is widely used in web development to build dynamic and interactive web applications. Its integration with the ASP.NET framework provides a robust environment for creating web solutions, including websites, e-commerce platforms, and content management systems.

Real-world examples of C# usage in web and application development include:

- E-commerce platforms: C# is utilized to develop robust e-commerce websites, enabling secure online transactions, inventory management, and seamless user experiences.

- Content management systems (CMS): C# powers popular CMS platforms like Umbraco, Sitecore, and Kentico, allowing developers to create and manage content-rich websites with ease.

- Financial applications: C# is employed to build financial applications such as online banking systems, stock trading platforms, and payment gateways.

Gaming and Virtual Reality

C# is a prevalent language in the gaming industry, particularly with the Unity game engine. Unity provides a powerful and user-friendly environment for developing games, and C# serves as the scripting language to create game mechanics, interactions, and behavior.

Real-world examples of C# usage in gaming and virtual reality include:

- Mobile games: C# is extensively used in developing mobile games for iOS and Android platforms, ranging from casual to high-performance and visually stunning games.

- Virtual reality (VR) and augmented reality (AR): C# is employed in creating immersive VR and AR experiences, allowing users to explore virtual worlds and interact with digital content.

Financial Services and Banking

The financial industry relies on robust and secure software solutions to manage transactions, risk, and customer data. C# is utilized in building financial systems that handle complex calculations, data analysis, and reporting.

Real-world examples of C# usage in financial services and banking include:

- Trading platforms: C# is employed in developing algorithmic trading systems, market data analysis tools, and trading execution platforms.

- Risk management systems: C# is utilized to build risk assessment and management applications, enabling financial institutions to identify, assess, and mitigate risks.

- Banking software: C# powers core banking systems, customer relationship management (CRM) platforms, and mobile banking applications.

Healthcare and Medical Technology

C# is increasingly utilized in healthcare and medical technology for building software solutions that enhance patient care, medical research, and data management. It enables developers to create secure and scalable applications compliant with regulatory standards.

Real-world examples of C# usage in healthcare and medical technology include:

- Electronic health records (EHR) systems: C# is employed in developing EHR platforms that centralize patient data, facilitate clinical workflows, and improve patient outcomes.

- Medical imaging and analysis software: C# is utilized to build applications for medical image processing, analysis, and visualization, aiding in diagnostic decision-making.

- Health monitoring and wearable devices: C# powers applications for health monitoring devices, wearables, and remote patient monitoring systems, enabling real-time data collection and analysis.

Chapter 7: Practicing and Improving Your C# Skills

Exploring Effective Ways to Practice and Improve C# Skills

Mastering any programming language requires continuous practice, hands-on experience, and a commitment to lifelong learning. In this chapter, we will delve into various strategies and techniques that will help you practice and improve your C# programming skills. By actively engaging in these methods, you will enhance your understanding of C#, strengthen your problem-solving abilities, and become a more confident and proficient C# developer.

Coding Challenges and Exercises

One of the most effective ways to improve your C# skills is by solving coding challenges and completing exercises specifically designed to enhance your understanding of key concepts. Online platforms such as LeetCode, HackerRank, and Codewars offer a wide range of C# coding challenges that cover various difficulty levels. These challenges require you to apply your knowledge of C# syntax, data structures, algorithms, and problem-solving techniques to solve real-world programming problems.

By regularly participating in coding challenges, you can:

- Develop a problem-solving mindset: Coding challenges present you with different problems and scenarios, forcing you to think critically and creatively to find solutions.

- Improve your algorithmic thinking: As you solve coding challenges, you will gain experience in developing efficient algorithms and optimizing your code for better performance.

- Familiarize yourself with common programming patterns: Coding challenges often require the implementation of common programming patterns such as recursion, dynamic programming, and graph traversal. By practicing these patterns, you will become more comfortable using them in real-world scenarios.

Personal Projects

Undertaking personal projects is an excellent way to apply your C# skills to real-world scenarios and gain hands-on experience. Personal projects allow you to explore your areas of interest, build practical applications, and showcase your abilities to potential employers or clients.

Consider the following when working on personal projects:

- Start with smaller, manageable projects: Begin with small projects that align with your skill level. This will enable you to complete them successfully and build confidence in your abilities. As you progress, gradually take on more complex projects that challenge you and push your boundaries.

- Use project-based learning: Structure your personal projects around specific goals and objectives. This approach allows you to focus on acquiring new skills or deepening your understanding of particular concepts while building a tangible application.

- Collaborate with others: Engaging in open-source projects or collaborating with fellow developers on personal projects can provide valuable learning opportunities. It allows you to learn from others, receive feedback on your code, and contribute to a larger project that benefits the community.

Reading and Studying C# Resources

Continuously expanding your knowledge through reading and studying C# resources is crucial for improving your skills. There are several resources available, including books, online tutorials, documentation, and blogs, that cover various aspects of C# programming.

Consider the following approaches when reading and studying C# resources:

- Choose reputable and up-to-date resources: Ensure that the resources you select are reliable, accurate, and reflect the current best practices in C# programming. Check reviews, recommendations, and publication dates to ensure you are accessing the most relevant information.

- Follow structured learning paths: Many online platforms offer structured learning paths or courses specifically designed to guide beginners in learning C#. Following these learning paths provides a comprehensive and organized approach to learning C#, covering essential topics and gradually building upon your knowledge.

- Practice alongside learning: While reading and studying, actively apply the concepts you learn by writing code and solving exercises. This practical application reinforces your understanding and helps solidify your knowledge.

Contributing to Open-Source Projects

Contributing to open-source projects not only enhances your C# skills but also allows you to collaborate with experienced developers and contribute to the larger software development community. Open-source projects provide opportunities to work on real-world codebases, understand industry best practices, and receive valuable feedback on your contributions.

Consider the following when contributing to open-source projects:

- Start with smaller tasks: Begin by tackling smaller issues or feature requests within the project. This allows you to familiarize yourself with the codebase, understand the project's development workflow, and gradually take on more significant tasks.

- Engage with the project community: Join the project's communication channels, such as forums or chat platforms, to interact with other contributors and seek guidance when needed. Building relationships within the community can provide valuable mentorship and networking opportunities.

- Follow contribution guidelines: Every open-source project has its own contribution guidelines. Familiarize yourself with these guidelines and ensure that you follow them when submitting your contributions. This demonstrates your professionalism and increases the chances of your contributions being accepted.

Suggestions for Projects and Exercises to Help Solidify Understanding

To solidify your understanding of C# programming and enhance your skills, it is essential to engage in practical projects and exercises. Applying your knowledge in real-world scenarios not only reinforces your understanding but also strengthens your problem-solving abilities and builds your confidence as a C# developer.

Build a Simple Calculator Application

A calculator application is a classic project that allows you to practice essential concepts such as variables, data types, operators, and control structures. Start by creating a basic console application that can perform basic arithmetic operations like addition, subtraction, multiplication, and division. As you progress, you can add more advanced features like handling decimal numbers, implementing error handling, or creating a graphical user interface (GUI) using frameworks like Windows Forms or WPF.

Develop a To do List Application

Creating a to do list application allows you to practice working with collections, loops, and conditional statements. Begin by designing a console-based application that allows users to add, delete, and update tasks. You can then expand on this project by implementing features like prioritizing tasks, sorting tasks based on due dates, and persisting the data using a database or file system.

Create a Contact Management System

A contact management system is a valuable project for practicing object-oriented programming (OOP) concepts. Design a program that enables users to create, edit, and search for contacts. Implement classes such as Contact, Address, and Phone Number, and establish relationships between them using concepts like inheritance, encapsulation, and polymorphism. Consider incorporating additional features such as importing and exporting contacts, displaying contact statistics, or implementing a graphical user interface.

Build a Basic Web Application

Expanding your skills to web development opens up a world of opportunities. Start by creating a simple web application using ASP.NET and C#. You can build a personal portfolio website, a blog, or a basic e-commerce site. Focus on implementing user authentication, database integration, and handling HTTP requests. As you become more comfortable, explore more advanced web development concepts like RESTful APIs, client-side frameworks, and responsive design.

Implement a Data Visualization Project

Data visualization is an essential skill for analyzing and presenting data effectively. Use libraries like Chart.js or D3.js along with C# to create interactive and visually appealing charts, graphs, or dashboards. You can work with real-world datasets or generate sample data to showcase your skills in data manipulation, data binding, and visual representation.

Participate in Coding Challenges and Competitions

Engaging in coding challenges and competitions provides an opportunity to sharpen your problem-solving skills and benchmark your abilities against other developers. Platforms like LeetCode, HackerRank, and Codeforces offer a variety of challenges categorized by difficulty levels. Solve problems related to algorithms, data structures, and programming paradigms, and strive to improve your efficiency and optimize your code.

Contribute to Open-Source Projects

Contributing to open-source projects allows you to collaborate with experienced developers, gain exposure to real-world codebases, and contribute to the open-source community. Choose a project aligned with your interests and skill level, and start by solving minor issues or adding new features. This provides practical experience in working with version control systems, understanding project workflows, and adhering to coding conventions.

Remember, the key to improving your C# skills is consistent practice and hands-on experience. Choose projects and exercises that challenge you, but are also within your reach. As you tackle these projects, don't hesitate to seek guidance from online resources, documentation, and developer communities. The process of building and refining your projects will deepen your understanding of C#, expose you to different programming scenarios, and help you develop the problem-solving skills required to succeed as a C# developer.

Book 2 - C# Programming: Intermediate Techniques and Frameworks

Introduction: Advancing in C#

Preparing for Advanced Topics in C#

As you progress in your journey to master C#, it is essential to prepare yourself for the advanced topics and techniques that will take your skills to the next level.

C# is a powerful programming language that offers a wide range of advanced features and frameworks. By mastering these advanced topics, you will unlock new possibilities and be able to develop more sophisticated applications with increased efficiency and flexibility.

Recognizing the Importance of Advancing in C#

Advancing in C# goes beyond just acquiring knowledge; it is about developing a deeper understanding of the language and its capabilities. By advancing in C#, you will:

- Enhance your problem-solving skills: Advanced topics in C# require you to think critically and creatively to find solutions to complex programming challenges. This will sharpen your problem-solving abilities and make you a more skilled developer.

- Increase your productivity: Advanced features and techniques in C# can significantly streamline your development process. By leveraging these tools effectively, you can write cleaner, more maintainable code and reduce development time.

- Expand your career opportunities: Proficiency in advanced C# concepts and frameworks opens doors to a wider range of job opportunities. Many industries, such as finance, healthcare, and gaming, require developers with expertise in advanced C# techniques.

Building a Strong Foundation

Before diving into advanced topics, it is crucial to have a solid understanding of the foundational concepts of C#. Ensure that you have a firm grasp of topics covered in earlier chapters, such as variables, data types, control flow, and object-oriented programming. This foundation will serve as a strong base upon which you can build your advanced C# skills.

Reviewing and Reinforcing Core Concepts

Before delving into advanced topics, take the time to review and reinforce your understanding of core concepts. This includes topics like exception handling, file I/O, LINQ (Language Integrated Query), and delegates. Brushing up on these topics will provide a solid framework for tackling more complex concepts.

Embracing Documentation and Official Resources

As you venture into more advanced C# topics, rely on official documentation and resources provided by Microsoft. The Microsoft Docs website offers comprehensive documentation, tutorials, and examples for various C# features and frameworks. These resources provide in-depth explanations and practical guidance to help you grasp complex concepts and apply them effectively.

Exploring Advanced Frameworks and Libraries

C# offers a rich ecosystem of advanced frameworks and libraries that can greatly enhance your development capabilities. In Book 2, we will explore frameworks like ASP.NET, which is widely used for building web applications. The use-cases at the end of each chapter in Book 2 will tie into a larger project titled "Developing an Inventory Management Web Application Using ASP.NET." This project will guide you through the process of building a comprehensive web-based inventory management system, allowing you to apply the advanced concepts learned in each chapter effectively.

Emphasizing Practical Application

To truly advance in C#, it is crucial to apply the knowledge gained through practical projects. As you progress through the chapters, complete the use-cases and exercises provided, and challenge yourself to create additional projects that showcase your understanding of the advanced concepts. Building real-world applications will solidify your understanding and demonstrate your proficiency to potential employers or clients.

Seeking Continuous Learning

Advancing in C# is an ongoing process. Technology evolves, new frameworks emerge, and best practices change. Embrace a mindset of continuous learning and stay updated with the latest developments in the C# ecosystem. Follow industry blogs, participate in developer communities, attend conferences, and explore online learning platforms to expand your knowledge and keep your skills sharp.

By preparing yourself for advanced topics in C#, you are setting yourself up for a rewarding and successful programming journey. Remember to build a strong foundation, review core concepts, explore advanced frameworks, and emphasize practical application. With dedication and a commitment to continuous learning, you will become a proficient and confident C# developer capable of tackling complex projects and advancing in your career.

Importance of Mastering Intermediate Topics in the C# Programming Journey

As you progress in your journey to become a proficient C# programmer, it is crucial to recognize the significance of mastering intermediate topics. Building upon the foundational knowledge you gained in earlier stages, mastering intermediate techniques and frameworks in C# will unlock a multitude of possibilities and propel you towards becoming a skilled developer.

Broadening Your Skill Set

Mastering intermediate topics in C# expands your repertoire of programming techniques and equips you with a broader range of tools to solve complex problems. By delving deeper into the language, you will gain expertise in advanced concepts, design patterns, and frameworks that are widely used in real-world applications. This broader skill set enables you to tackle more sophisticated projects and opens doors to a wider array of career opportunities.

Enhancing Problem-Solving Abilities

The intermediate topics in C# challenge you to think critically and creatively to solve intricate programming puzzles. These topics often involve more complex algorithms, data structures, and design patterns. By mastering these techniques, you will sharpen your problem-solving abilities, enabling you to approach challenges with a strategic mindset and craft elegant solutions.

Increasing Productivity and Efficiency

Intermediate topics in C# introduce you to advanced language features, frameworks, and tools that enhance your productivity and efficiency as a developer. For instance, learning about advanced data structures and algorithms allows you to optimize the performance of your code, resulting in faster and more efficient programs. Additionally, mastering frameworks like ASP.NET empowers you to build robust web applications with less effort and time.

Developing Scalable and Maintainable Code

As you progress in C#, you will encounter topics such as software architecture, design patterns, and code organization. These intermediate concepts teach you how to write modular, reusable, and maintainable code. By understanding these principles, you can develop scalable applications that can adapt to changing requirements and are easier to maintain and extend over time.

Expanding Application Development Possibilities

Mastering intermediate topics in C# introduces you to various frameworks and libraries that expand the scope of application development. For example, learning about Windows Presentation Foundation (WPF) allows you to create rich desktop applications with intuitive user interfaces. Exploring Xamarin enables you to develop cross-platform mobile applications. These intermediate topics equip you with the knowledge and skills to explore different domains and cater to a broader audience.

Realizing the Potential of Advanced Projects

The use-cases at the end of each chapter in Book 2 tie into a larger project titled "Developing an Inventory Management Web Application Using ASP.NET." This comprehensive project serves as a culmination of the knowledge gained throughout the book, integrating various aspects of intermediate techniques and frameworks. By embarking on this project, you will apply your newfound skills to a complex real-world scenario, gaining practical experience and showcasing your capabilities to potential employers or clients.

Chapter 1: C# Data Structures and Algorithms

Explanation and Usage of Various Data Structures in C#

Data structures play a crucial role in programming as they provide efficient ways to organize and manipulate data. In this chapter, we will explore various data structures available in C# and delve into their explanations and usage. Understanding these data structures will empower you to write more efficient and scalable code, improving the performance and functionality of your C# programs.

Arrays

An array is a fixed-size, sequential collection of elements of the same type. The elements in an array can be accessed directly using an index. Arrays are useful when you know the size of the collection in advance and need fast access to its elements. Here's an example of how to declare, initialize, and use an array in C#:

int[] numbers = new int[5] {1, 2, 3, 4, 5};

Console.WriteLine(numbers[0]); // Output: 1

Lists

The **List<T>** class is a generic class that represents a resizable array. It provides methods to search, sort, and manipulate lists. Lists are useful when you need a collection that can change in size. Here's an example:

List<int> numbers = new List<int> {1, 2, 3, 4, 5};

numbers.Add(6); // Add an element to the list

Console.WriteLine(numbers[5]); // Output: 6

Stacks

The **Stack<T>** class represents a last-in, first-out (LIFO) collection of objects. It provides methods to push (add) items, pop (remove) items, and peek (look at the top item without removing it). Stacks are useful for things like backtracking algorithms and balancing symbols in a parser. Here is the example:

Stack<int> stack = new Stack<int>();

stack.Push(1); // Add an element to the stack

stack.Push(2);

Console.WriteLine(stack.Pop()); // Remove and return the top element. Output: 2

Queues

The **Queue<T>** class represents a first-in, first-out (FIFO) collection of objects. It provides methods to enqueue (add) items, dequeue (remove) items, and peek (look at the first item without removing it). Queues are useful for things like task scheduling and buffering data streams. Here is the example:

Queue<int> queue = new Queue<int>();

queue.Enqueue(1); // Add an element to the queue

queue.Enqueue(2);

Console.WriteLine(queue.Dequeue()); // Remove and return the first element. Output: 1

Linked Lists

The **LinkedList<T>** class represents a doubly-linked list. It provides methods to add, remove, and search items in the list. Linked lists are useful when you need to frequently add or remove items from the middle of the collection. Here is the example:

LinkedList<int> linkedList = new LinkedList<int>();

linkedList.AddLast(1); // Add an element to the end of the list

linkedList.AddLast(2);

Console.WriteLine(linkedList.First.Value); // Output: 1

HashSets

The **HashSet<T>** class represents a set of unique elements. It provides methods to add, remove, and check if an item exists in the set. HashSets are useful when you need to quickly check if an item is part of a collection, and you don't care about the order of the items. Here is the example:

HashSet<int> set = new HashSet<int>();

set.Add(1); // Add an element to the set

set.Add(2);

Console.WriteLine(set.Contains(1)); // Check if an element exists. Output: True

Dictionaries

The **Dictionary<TKey, TValue>** class represents a collection of keys and values. It provides methods to add, remove, and find items based on their key. Dictionaries are useful when you need to associate values with keys, and you need to retrieve values based on their keys. Here is the example:

Dictionary<string, int> dictionary = new Dictionary<string, int>();

dictionary["one"] = 1; // Add a key/value pair to the dictionary

dictionary["two"] = 2;

Console.WriteLine(dictionary["one"]); // Output: 1

SortedSet and SortedList

The **SortedSet<T>** and **SortedList<TKey, TValue>** classes represent collections that are always sorted. **SortedSet<T>** is a collection of unique elements, and **SortedList<TKey, TValue>** is a collection of key/value pairs. They are useful when you need to maintain a sorted collection. Here is an example.

SortedSet<int> sortedSet = new SortedSet<int> {2, 1, 3};

Console.WriteLine(sortedSet.Min); // Output: 1

SortedList<string, int> sortedList = new SortedList<string, int> {{"two", 2}, {"one", 1}, {"three", 3}};

Console.WriteLine(sortedList.Keys[0]); // Output: one

Each of these data structures has its strengths and weaknesses, and the choice of which one to use depends on the specific requirements of your program. Understanding these data structures and their properties can help you choose the right one for your needs and write more efficient code.

Implementing Common Algorithms in C#

Algorithms form the foundation of efficient and optimized programming. They provide step-by-step instructions for solving problems and manipulating data structures. In this section, we will explore the implementation of common algorithms in C# and understand their applications in various scenarios. By mastering these algorithms, you will gain the skills needed to write elegant and efficient code that can handle complex tasks and improve the performance of your C# programs.

Sorting Algorithms

These algorithms are used to rearrange a given array or list elements according to a comparison operator on the elements. The comparison operator is used to decide the new order of element in the respective data structure.

- **Bubble Sort**: Bubble Sort is the simplest sorting algorithm that works by repeatedly swapping the adjacent elements if they are in the wrong order. It's best used for small lists or for lists that are already mostly sorted.

- **Selection Sort**: This sorting algorithm sorts an array by repeatedly finding the minimum element from unsorted part and putting it at the beginning. It's not suitable for large lists, as it's not very efficient.

- **Insertion Sort**: Insertion sort is a simple sorting algorithm that works the way we sort playing cards in our hands. It's efficient for smaller lists, and for lists that are already mostly sorted.

- **Quick Sort**: QuickSort is a Divide and Conquer algorithm that picks an element as pivot and partitions the given array around the picked pivot. It's one of the most efficient and commonly-used sorting algorithms.

- **Merge Sort**: MergeSort is also a Divide and Conquer algorithm. It divides the input array into two halves, calls itself for the two halves, and then merges the two sorted halves. It's very efficient but requires additional space equal to the array being sorted.

Below is the example of how to implement selection sort.

```
public static void SelectionSort(int[] arr)
{
    for (int i = 0; i < arr.Length - 1; i++)
    {
        int minIndex = i;
        for (int j = i + 1; j < arr.Length; j++)
        {
            if (arr[j] < arr[minIndex])
            {
                minIndex = j;
            }
        }
        int temp = arr[minIndex];
        arr[minIndex] = arr[i];
        arr[i] = temp;
    }
}
```

Searching Algorithms

These algorithms are designed to check for an element or retrieve an element from any data structure where it is stored.

- **Linear Search**: Linear search is a very simple search algorithm. In this type of search, a sequential search is made over all items one by one. Every item is checked and if a match is found then that particular item is returned, otherwise the search continues till the end of the data structure.

- **Binary Search**: Binary search looks for a particular item by comparing the middle most item of the collection. If a match occurs, then the index of item is returned. If the middle item is greater than the item, then the item is searched in the sub-array to the left of the middle item. Otherwise, the item is searched for in the sub-array to the right of the middle item. This process continues on the sub-array as well until the size of the subarray reduces to zero.

Below is the example of how to implement linear search.

```
public static int LinearSearch(int[] arr, int key)
{
    for (int i = 0; i < arr.Length; i++)
    {
        if (arr[i] == key)
        {
            return i;
        }
    }
    return -1;
}
```

Graph Algorithms

These algorithms are designed to solve problems by modeling the problem as a graph.

- **Depth-First Search (DFS)**: DFS is a traversal algorithm that uses a stack to explore as far as possible along each branch before backtracking. It's often used for tasks such as checking connectedness of a graph and testing if a graph is a tree.

- **Breadth-First Search (BFS)**: BFS is another traversal algorithm that uses a queue to explore all of a vertex's neighbors before moving on to their neighbors. It's often used for finding the shortest path in a graph and for testing if a graph is bipartite.

- **Dijkstra's Algorithm**: This is a shortest-path algorithm for weighted graphs. It finds the shortest path from a starting vertex to all other vertices in the graph.

Below is the example of how to implement Depth-First Search (DFS):

```
// This is a simplified example. A real-world DFS would require a more complex implementation.
public static void DFS(int[][] graph, bool[] visited, int node)
{
    if (visited[node])
    {
        return;
    }

    visited[node] = true;

    foreach (var neighbour in graph[node])
    {
        DFS(graph, visited, neighbour);
    }
}
```

Dynamic Programming

Dynamic programming is a method for solving complex problems by breaking them down into simpler subproblems. It's used when the subproblems overlap, i.e., when the same subproblem is solved multiple times.

- **Fibonacci Sequence**: The Fibonacci sequence is a classic example of a problem that can be solved using dynamic programming. The sequence is defined as: fib(0) = 0, fib(1) = 1, fib(n) = fib(n-1) + fib(n-2) for n > 1. A simple recursive solution has exponential time complexity, but dynamic programming provides a polynomial time solution.

- **Knapsack Problem**: The knapsack problem is a problem in combinatorial optimization. Given a set of items, each with a weight and a value, determine the number of each item to include in a collection so that the total weight is less than or equal to a given limit and the total value is as large as possible.

Below is the example of how to implement Fibonacci Sequence:

```
public static int Fibonacci(int n)
```

```
{
    int[] fib = new int[n + 2];
    fib[0] = 0;
    fib[1] = 1;

    for (int i = 2; i <= n; i++)
    {
        fib[i] = fib[i - 1] + fib[i - 2];
    }

    return fib[n];
}
```

Recursion

Recursion is a method where the solution to a problem depends on solutions to smaller instances of the same problem.

- **Factorial Calculation**: The factorial of a non-negative integer n is the product of all positive integers less than or equal to n. It can be calculated using recursion as: fact(n) = n * fact(n-1) for n > 0 and fact(0) = 1.

- **Tower of Hanoi**: The Tower of Hanoi is a mathematical game or puzzle. It consists of three rods and a number of disks of different sizes, which can slide onto any rod. The puzzle starts with the disks in a neat stack in ascending order of size on one rod, the smallest at the top. The objective of the puzzle is to move the entire stack to another rod, obeying the following simple rules: (1) Only one disk can be moved at a time. (2) Each move consists of taking the upper disk from one of the stacks and placing it on top of another stack or on an empty rod. (3) No disk may be placed on top of a smaller disk.

Below is the example of how to implement Factorial Calculation:

```
public static int Factorial(int number)
{
    if (number == 0)
```

```
    return 1;
  return number * Factorial(number - 1);
}
```

Greedy Algorithms

A greedy algorithm is an algorithmic paradigm that follows the problem-solving heuristic of making the locally optimal choice at each stage with the hope of finding a global optimum.

- **Activity Selection Problem**: The problem is to select the maximum number of activities that can be performed by a single person or machine, assuming that a person can only work on a single activity at a time. The greedy choice is to always pick the next activity whose finish time is least among the remaining activities and the start time is more than or equal to the finish time of the previously selected activity.

- **Kruskal's Minimum Spanning Tree (MST)**: Kruskal's MST is a greedy algorithm to find the minimum spanning tree of a graph. The greedy choice is to pick the smallest weight edge that does not cause a cycle in the MST constructed so far.

- **Coin Change Problem**: Given a set of coin denominations, find the minimum number of coins required to make a specific amount of change.

Below is the example of how to implement Coin Change Problem:

```
public static int CoinChange(int[] coins, int amount)
{
  Array.Sort(coins);
  int count = 0;
  for (int i = coins.Length - 1; i >= 0; i--)
  {
    while (amount >= coins[i])
    {
      amount -= coins[i];
      count++;
    }
  }
```

```
return amount == 0 ? count : -1;
}
```

These are just a few examples of the many algorithms that fall under these categories. Each algorithm has its own strengths and weaknesses, and the choice of which one to use depends on the specific needs of your program.

Building Use Case: Designing a Sorting Algorithm

Sorting algorithms are an essential part of programming and play a crucial role in organizing and arranging data in a specific order. In this section, we will explore a practical use case that focuses on designing a sorting algorithm using C#. By working through this use case, you will gain a deeper understanding of how sorting algorithms function and how to implement them effectively in your own projects.

The goal of designing a sorting algorithm is to arrange a collection of elements in a specific order, such as ascending or descending. This is particularly useful when dealing with large datasets or when you need to present information in a structured and organized manner. Sorting algorithms can be applied to various scenarios, such as organizing customer data, arranging scores in a leaderboard, or ordering a list of products based on specific criteria.

let's walk through the process of implementing a simple sorting algorithm in C#. We'll use the Bubble Sort algorithm for this example, as it's one of the simplest sorting algorithms to understand and implement.

Step 1: Understand the Algorithm

Bubble Sort works by repeatedly swapping the adjacent elements if they are in the wrong order. This process continues until no more swaps are needed, indicating that the list is sorted.

Step 2: Set Up Your Development Environment

To write and run C# code, you need a development environment. If you don't have one set up yet, you can install Visual Studio, which is a popular IDE for C# development. You can download it from the official Microsoft website.

Step 3: Create a New Console Application

Once you have Visual Studio installed, open it and create a new Console App (.NET Core) project. Name it "BubbleSort".

Step 4: Implement the Bubble Sort Algorithm

Open the Program.cs file and replace the existing code with the following:

```
using System;

class Program
{
    static void Main()
    {
        int[] arr = {64, 34, 25, 12, 22, 11, 90};
        Console.WriteLine("Unsorted array:");
        PrintArray(arr);

        BubbleSort(arr);

        Console.WriteLine("Sorted array:");
        PrintArray(arr);
    }

    static void BubbleSort(int[] arr)
    {
        int n = arr.Length;
        for (int i = 0; i < n - 1; i++)
        {
            for (int j = 0; j < n - i - 1; j++)
            {
```

```csharp
        if (arr[j] > arr[j + 1])

        {

            // Swap arr[j] and arr[j+1]

            int temp = arr[j];

            arr[j] = arr[j + 1];

            arr[j + 1] = temp;

        }

      }

    }

}


static void PrintArray(int[] arr)

{

    int n = arr.Length;

    for (int i = 0; i < n; ++i)

        Console.Write(arr[i] + " ");

    Console.WriteLine();

  }

}
```

Step 5: Run the Program

Press F5 or click the "Start Debugging" button to run the program. You should see the unsorted and sorted arrays printed to the console.

Step 6: Experiment and Learn

Try modifying the array or implementing a different sorting algorithm. The more you experiment and practice, the better you'll understand how these algorithms work.

Remember, this is a basic implementation of the Bubble Sort algorithm. There are many other sorting algorithms out there, each with its own strengths and weaknesses. As you learn more about programming and algorithms, you'll start to understand when to use each one.

Chapter 2: Object-Oriented Programming in C#

Understanding OOP Principles in the Context of C#

Object-Oriented Programming (OOP) is a powerful paradigm that allows developers to organize and structure their code in a more modular and reusable way. In this chapter, we will explore the fundamental principles of OOP in the context of C#. By understanding these principles, you will be able to design and implement robust and maintainable C# applications.

Encapsulation

Encapsulation is the principle of bundling related data and behavior into a single unit called a class. In C#, a class serves as a blueprint for creating objects. It encapsulates the data (attributes or properties) and methods (behavior) that operate on that data. Encapsulation promotes code organization, data hiding, and modularity, allowing for better code maintenance and reusability.

Inheritance

Inheritance is a mechanism that allows a class to inherit properties and behaviors from another class. In C#, you can create a hierarchy of classes where subclasses inherit characteristics from their parent or base class. Inheritance promotes code reuse, as you can define common attributes and methods in a base class and extend or specialize them in derived classes. It enables the creation of more specialized classes while maintaining a structured and organized codebase.

Polymorphism

Polymorphism is the ability of an object to take on many forms. In C#, polymorphism can be achieved through method overriding and method overloading. Method overriding allows a derived class to provide its own implementation of a method defined in the base class, while method overloading allows multiple methods with the same name but different parameters to coexist. Polymorphism enables flexibility and extensibility in code, as objects of different classes can be treated interchangeably based on their common interfaces or base classes.

Understanding these OOP principles in the context of C# empowers you to create more flexible and maintainable code. By encapsulating related data and behavior into classes, leveraging inheritance to create class hierarchies, and utilizing polymorphism to handle objects in a more generic way, you can build scalable and extensible applications.

Examples of OOP Implementation in C#

Object-Oriented Programming (OOP) provides a powerful framework for structuring code and building modular applications. In this chapter, we will explore practical examples of OOP implementation in C#. By examining real-world scenarios, you will gain a deeper understanding of how to apply OOP principles effectively.

Class Inheritance

One of the key features of OOP is class inheritance. In C#, you can create derived classes that inherit properties and behaviors from a base class. For example, consider a scenario where you are developing a software application for a car dealership. You can define a base class called "Vehicle," which includes common attributes and methods shared by all vehicles, such as "Make," "Model," and "StartEngine()." Then, you can create derived classes like "Car" and "Motorcycle" that inherit from the "Vehicle" class and add their own specific attributes and methods. This inheritance hierarchy promotes code reuse and allows you to manage related objects efficiently.

Encapsulation and Abstraction

Encapsulation and abstraction are essential concepts in OOP. Encapsulation involves bundling related data and behavior within a class, while abstraction focuses on exposing only relevant information to the outside world. For instance, imagine you are developing a banking application. You can create a class called "BankAccount" that encapsulates attributes like "AccountNumber" and "Balance" and methods like "Deposit()" and "Withdraw()." By encapsulating these details, you can hide the internal workings of the account and provide a simplified interface for interacting with it. This encapsulation and abstraction allow for better code organization, maintainability, and reusability.

Polymorphism

Polymorphism is another powerful feature of OOP. It enables objects of different classes to be treated interchangeably based on their common interfaces or base classes. In C#, you can achieve polymorphism through method overriding and interfaces. For example, let's say you are developing a software application for a university. You can define a base class called "Person" with a method called "PrintDetails()." Then, you can create derived classes like "Student" and "Professor" that override the "PrintDetails()" method with their own implementation. By treating objects of both classes as "Person" objects, you can invoke the "PrintDetails()" method and obtain polymorphic behavior. This flexibility allows for code extensibility and adaptability.

These examples highlight the practical application of OOP principles in C#. By leveraging class inheritance, encapsulation, abstraction, and polymorphism, you can create well-structured and maintainable code.

Building Use Case: Implementing an Inventory System

We will delve into a practical use case that involves implementing an inventory system using object-oriented programming (OOP) principles in C#. This project will provide hands-on experience and showcase how to apply the concepts learned to solve a real-world problem.

An inventory system is crucial for businesses to efficiently manage their stock, track inventory levels, and handle various operations such as adding new items, updating quantities, and generating reports. By developing an inventory system, you will gain a deeper understanding of how to design classes, utilize inheritance, encapsulate data, and leverage other OOP features in a meaningful way.

let's walk through the process of implementing a simple inventory system in C#. This system will allow you to add items to the inventory, remove items from the inventory, and check the quantity of a specific item.

Step 1: Understand the Problem

The problem is to create an inventory system that can keep track of various items and their quantities.

Step 2: Design the Classes

We'll need two classes for this system: Item and Inventory.

The **Item** class will represent an individual item. It will have properties for the item's name and quantity.

The **Inventory** class will represent the inventory itself. It will have a method to add items, a method to remove items, and a method to check the quantity of a specific item.

Step 3: Set Up Your Development Environment

To write and run C# code, you need a development environment. If you don't have one set up yet, you can install Visual Studio, which is a popular IDE for C# development. You can download it from the official Microsoft website.

Step 4: Create a New Console Application

Once you have Visual Studio installed, open it and create a new Console App (.NET Core) project. Name it "InventorySystem".

Step 5: Implement the Classes

Open the Program.cs file and replace the existing code with the following:

```
using System;
using System.Collections.Generic;


public class Item
{
    public string Name { get; set; }
    public int Quantity { get; set; }
}


public class Inventory
```

```
{
    private List<Item> items = new List<Item>();


    public void AddItem(string name, int quantity)
    {
        items.Add(new Item { Name = name, Quantity = quantity });
    }


    public void RemoveItem(string name)
    {
        Item itemToRemove = items.Find(item => item.Name == name);
        if (itemToRemove != null)
        {
            items.Remove(itemToRemove);
        }
    }


    public int CheckQuantity(string name)
    {
        Item item = items.Find(i => i.Name == name);
        return item != null ? item.Quantity : 0;
    }
}


class Program
{
    static void Main()
    {
        Inventory inventory = new Inventory();
```

```
inventory.AddItem("Apple", 10);

inventory.AddItem("Banana", 20);

Console.WriteLine(inventory.CheckQuantity("Apple")); // Output: 10

inventory.RemoveItem("Apple");

Console.WriteLine(inventory.CheckQuantity("Apple")); // Output: 0

    }

}
```

Step 6: Run the Program

Press F5 or click the "Start Debugging" button to run the program. You should see the quantity of "Apple" printed as 10, then as 0 after it's removed from the inventory.

Step 7: Experiment and Learn

Try modifying the program to add more features. For example, you could add a method to the **Inventory** class to list all items in the inventory, or you could add a method to update the quantity of an existing item. The more you experiment and practice, the better you'll understand how to use object-oriented programming in C#.

Chapter 3: C# Frameworks and Libraries

Introduction to Popular C# Frameworks and Libraries

We will explore some of the popular frameworks and libraries available in the C# ecosystem. These frameworks and libraries provide developers with pre-built tools, functionalities, and components that can significantly streamline the development process and enhance the capabilities of C# applications.

ASP.NET

ASP.NET is a widely-used web application framework developed by Microsoft. It provides a robust and scalable platform for building dynamic websites, web APIs, and web applications. ASP.NET includes features like server controls, data binding, authentication, and session management, making it a powerful framework for web development.

Entity Framework

Entity Framework (EF) is an object-relational mapping (ORM) framework that simplifies database access and manipulation in C#. It provides a high-level abstraction over database operations, allowing developers to work with entities and relationships rather than dealing with low-level SQL queries. EF supports various database providers and enables rapid development and maintenance of data-driven applications.

WPF

Windows Presentation Foundation (WPF) is a framework for building desktop applications with rich user interfaces. It provides a flexible and powerful set of tools for designing and developing visually appealing applications. WPF leverages XAML (eXtensible Application Markup Language) for UI design and supports features like data binding, styling, animation, and multimedia integration.

Xamarin

Xamarin is a cross-platform development framework that allows developers to build native mobile applications for iOS, Android, and Windows using C#. It provides a shared codebase, allowing developers to write the majority of their application logic in C# and reuse it across multiple platforms. Xamarin ensures native performance and access to platform-specific APIs, resulting in high-quality mobile applications.

NUnit

NUnit is a popular unit testing framework for C#. It provides a comprehensive set of tools and attributes for writing and executing unit tests. With NUnit, developers can create automated tests to verify the correctness of their code, identify bugs, and ensure the reliability of their applications. Unit testing is a critical practice for maintaining code quality and facilitating future enhancements.

Moq

Moq is a mocking framework for C#, used primarily in unit testing. It allows developers to create mock objects that simulate the behavior of dependencies or external components, enabling isolated and controlled testing scenarios. Moq simplifies the process of setting up test cases, defining expectations, and verifying interactions with dependencies.

SignalR

SignalR is a real-time communication framework for building interactive web applications. It enables bi-directional communication between the server and client, allowing real-time updates and notifications. With SignalR, developers can create responsive and dynamic applications, such as chat systems, live dashboards, and collaborative tools.

By familiarizing yourself with these frameworks and libraries, you can leverage their capabilities and accelerate your development process. Each framework has its own strengths and is suited for specific use cases, so it's essential to choose the right one based on your project requirements.

Remember to stay updated with the latest releases and developments in these frameworks and libraries, as the technology landscape evolves rapidly. By continuously learning and exploring new possibilities, you can stay at the forefront of C# development and deliver innovative solutions to meet the demands of modern software development.

Examples of How to Use These Tools to Enhance C# Development

In the previous section, we explored some popular frameworks and libraries in the C# ecosystem. Now, let's dive deeper into how these tools can be used to enhance C# development and empower developers to build more robust and efficient applications. By leveraging the capabilities of these frameworks and libraries, developers can streamline their workflow, reduce development time, and create high-quality software solutions.

1. ASP.NET: With ASP.NET, developers can take advantage of its extensive set of features to build powerful web applications. By using server controls, developers can easily create interactive user interfaces and handle user input effectively. Additionally, ASP.NET's data binding capabilities enable seamless integration with databases, simplifying data retrieval and manipulation. The framework also offers authentication and authorization mechanisms, ensuring secure access to web applications. By mastering ASP.NET, developers can create dynamic and feature-rich web applications that cater to a wide range of user needs.

   Here's a simple example of an ASP.NET MVC controller:

   ```
   public class HomeController : Controller
   {
       public ActionResult Index()
       {
           return View();
       }
   }
   ```

2. Entity Framework: Entity Framework provides a convenient and efficient way to work with databases in C#. It abstracts away the complexities of database operations by mapping database entities to C# objects. With Entity Framework, developers can focus on writing code that interacts with entities, eliminating the need for manual SQL queries. By leveraging the power of Entity Framework's LINQ (Language Integrated Query), developers can perform complex database queries and manipulations using a familiar

syntax. This simplifies data access and enhances productivity in database-driven applications.

Here's an example of how to define a model and query the database:

```
public class Blog
{
    public int BlogId { get; set; }
    public string Url { get; set; }
}


public class BloggingContext : DbContext
{
    public DbSet<Blog> Blogs { get; set; }
}


// Querying the database
using (var db = new BloggingContext())
{
    var blogs = db.Blogs
        .Where(b => b.Url.Contains("dotnet"))
        .ToList();
}
```

3. WPF: Windows Presentation Foundation (WPF) enables developers to build visually appealing desktop applications with rich user interfaces. With WPF, developers can create stunning UI designs using XAML (eXtensible Application Markup Language) and leverage a variety of controls and layout options. The framework supports data binding, allowing developers to bind UI elements directly to data sources. This facilitates the automatic updating of UI elements when data changes, resulting in a more responsive and interactive user experience. WPF also provides advanced features like animations, styles, and templates, enabling developers to create highly customizable and visually engaging applications.

Here's an example of a simple WPF application:

XML

```xml
<Window x:Class="WpfApp.MainWindow"
    xmlns="http://schemas.microsoft.com/winfx/2006/xaml/presentation"
    xmlns:x="http://schemas.microsoft.com/winfx/2006/xaml"
    Title="MainWindow" Height="350" Width="525">
  <Grid>
    <Button Content="Click me" HorizontalAlignment="Left" Margin="10,10,0,0"
VerticalAlignment="Top" Width="75" Click="Button_Click"/>
  </Grid>
</Window>
```

C#

```csharp
public partial class MainWindow : Window
{
    public MainWindow()
    {
        InitializeComponent();
    }

    private void Button_Click(object sender, RoutedEventArgs e)
    {
        MessageBox.Show("Hello, WPF!");
    }
}
```

4. Xamarin: Xamarin is a powerful cross-platform framework that allows developers to write native mobile applications using C#. By sharing code across different platforms, developers can significantly reduce development time and effort. Xamarin provides access to native APIs, ensuring that the resulting applications deliver the same performance and user experience as their platform-specific counterparts. With Xamarin, developers can

build mobile apps for iOS, Android, and Windows platforms, reaching a broader audience with a single codebase.

Here's an example of a simple Xamarin.Forms page:

```csharp
public class MainPage : ContentPage
{
    public MainPage()
    {
        Content = new StackLayout
        {
            Children = {
                new Label { Text = "Hello, Xamarin!" }
            }
        };
    }
}
```

5. NUnit: NUnit is a widely used unit testing framework for C#. By writing unit tests using NUnit, developers can verify the correctness of their code, detect bugs early in the development process, and ensure the overall stability of their applications. NUnit provides various testing assertions and utilities, making it easy to define test cases, perform assertions, and generate meaningful test reports. With a solid understanding of NUnit, developers can adopt a test-driven development approach and confidently refactor their code while maintaining code quality.

Here's an example of a simple NUnit test:

```csharp
[TestFixture]
public class ExampleTests
{
    [Test]
    public void AdditionTest()
    {
```

```
    Assert.AreEqual(4, 2 + 2);

    }

}
```

6. Moq: Moq is a popular mocking framework that simplifies the testing of dependencies in C# applications. It allows developers to create mock objects that simulate the behavior of dependencies during unit testing. By using Moq, developers can isolate specific components of their applications, ensuring that they are thoroughly tested in isolation. This leads to more reliable and maintainable code by eliminating unwanted dependencies and ensuring proper encapsulation.

Here's an example of how to use Moq to create a mock object for a unit test:

```
public interface IFoo

{

    string Bar();

}


[Test]

public void MoqTest()

{

    var mock = new Mock<IFoo>();

    mock.Setup(foo => foo.Bar()).Returns("Mocked!");


    Assert.AreEqual("Mocked!", mock.Object.Bar());

}
```

7. SignalR: SignalR is a real-time communication framework for building interactive web applications. It facilitates bidirectional communication between the server and client, enabling real-time updates and notifications. SignalR is particularly useful in applications that require live data updates, such as chat applications, collaborative tools, and real-time monitoring systems. By incorporating SignalR into their C# applications, developers can create highly interactive and responsive user experiences.

Here's an example of a SignalR hub:

```
public class ChatHub : Hub

{

    public async Task SendMessage(string user, string message)

    {

        await Clients.All.SendAsync("ReceiveMessage", user, message);

    }

}
```

These are just simple examples. Each of these tools is quite powerful and can be used to build complex applications.

Building Use Case: Building a Basic Web App with ASP.NET

We will explore a practical use case to demonstrate how to build a basic web application using ASP.NET, one of the popular frameworks in the C# ecosystem. By following this use case, readers will gain hands-on experience and learn the essential concepts required to develop web applications using ASP.NET.

Building a web application involves various components such as user interfaces, data storage, and business logic. ASP.NET provides a robust foundation for developing web applications by offering a comprehensive set of tools and features. Let's walk through the steps involved in building a basic web app using ASP.NET. This application will be a simple "Hello, World!" web app.

Step 1: Set Up Your Development Environment

To write and run ASP.NET Core code, you need a development environment. If you don't have one set up yet, you can install Visual Studio, which is a popular IDE for C# development. You can download it from the official Microsoft website.

Step 2: Create a New ASP.NET Core Web Application

Once you have Visual Studio installed, open it and create a new ASP.NET Core Web Application project. Name it "HelloWorld".

Step 3: Choose the Web Application Template

In the "New ASP.NET Core Web Application" dialog, choose the "Web Application" template, which creates a project with a simple UI and support for Razor Pages.

Step 4: Implement the Web Application

Open the **Index.cshtml** file under the **Pages** folder and replace the existing code with the following:

XML

```
@page
@model IndexModel
@{
    ViewData["Title"] = "Home page";
}


<div class="text-center">
    <h1 class="display-4">Hello, World!</h1>
</div>
```

This code will display a "Hello, World!" message on the home page of your web application.

Step 5: Run the Web Application

Press F5 or click the "Start Debugging" button to run the web application. Your default web browser should open and display the "Hello, World!" message.

Step 6: Experiment and Learn

Try modifying the web application to add more features. For example, you could add a form to the home page that allows users to enter their name, and then display a personalized greeting message. The more you experiment and practice, the better you'll understand how to use ASP.NET Core to build web applications.

Chapter 4: Practical C# Projects

Practical Projects That Illustrate C# Capabilities

We will explore practical projects that showcase the capabilities of C# programming. These projects will provide hands-on experience and help readers solidify their understanding of C# concepts and techniques learned throughout the book.

Contact Management Application

Build a contact management application that allows users to store and manage their contacts. The application should provide features such as adding new contacts, searching and filtering contacts, and updating contact information. Implement various C# concepts such as classes, objects, collections, and file handling to create a functional and user-friendly contact management system.

Text-based Game

Create a text-based game using C# that engages users with interactive storytelling. The game can be a simple adventure or a role-playing game where users make choices that affect the outcome. Implement game mechanics such as character creation, decision-making, and branching storylines using C# programming constructs like conditionals, loops, and data structures.

Calculator Application

Develop a calculator application that performs basic arithmetic operations. The application should have a graphical user interface (GUI) and support addition, subtraction, multiplication, and division. Implement event handling, user input validation, and mathematical operations using C# to create a functional and intuitive calculator tool.

Weather Forecast Application

Build a weather forecast application that retrieves and displays weather information for a specified location. Utilize APIs (Application Programming Interfaces) to fetch real-time weather data from external sources and present it in a user-friendly format. Implement features such as location search, data parsing, and data visualization using C# to create a practical weather forecasting tool.

File Management System

Develop a file management system that allows users to organize and manage files and folders on their computer. The application should provide functionalities like creating new folders, moving and renaming files, and searching for specific files. Use C# file handling capabilities, directory operations, and user interface design to create an efficient and user-friendly file management system.

Image Processing Tool

Create an image processing tool that enables users to perform basic image editing operations. Implement features such as cropping, resizing, applying filters, and adjusting color settings. Utilize C# libraries and frameworks for image processing to build a versatile and user-friendly image editing tool.

By working on these practical projects, readers will gain hands-on experience in applying C# concepts and techniques to real-world scenarios. These projects will reinforce their understanding of C# capabilities and help them develop practical problem-solving skills.

Step-By-Step Guides for Building These Projects

These guides will walk you through the process of creating each project, starting from the initial setup to the final implementation. By following these guides, you will gain hands-on experience and deepen your understanding of intermediate C# techniques and frameworks.

Contact Management Application

- **Step 1**: Define a **Contact** class with properties like **FirstName**, **LastName**, **Phone Number**, **Email**, etc.

- **Step 2**: Create a **ContactManager** class that will hold a **List<Contact>** and methods to **AddContact**, **RemoveContact**, **SearchContact**, etc.

- **Step 3**: In your **Main** method, create an instance of **ContactManager** and a user interface (probably console-based) that allows the user to add, remove, and search contacts.

Text-based Game

- **Step 1**: Define classes for **Character**, **Item**, **Location**, etc. Each class should have properties and methods relevant to what it represents.

- **Step 2**: Create a **GameEngine** class that controls the game logic. This class should have methods to start the game, handle user input, and update the game state.

- **Step 3**: In your **Main** method, create an instance of **GameEngine** and start the game.

Calculator Application

- **Step 1**: Create a **Calculator** class with methods for each operation you want to support (e.g., **Add**, **Subtract**, **Multiply**, **Divide**).

- **Step 2**: In your **Main** method, create a user interface (probably console-based) that allows the user to enter numbers and choose an operation. Then, call the appropriate method on your **Calculator** instance and display the result.

Weather Forecast Application

- **Step 1**: Choose a weather API (like OpenWeatherMap) and find out how to make requests to it in C#.

- **Step 2**: Create a **WeatherService** class that makes requests to the weather API and returns the results.

- **Step 3**: In your **Main** method, create an instance of **WeatherService** and a user interface that allows the user to enter a location and displays the weather forecast for that location.

File Management System

- **Step 1**: Create a **FileManager** class with methods to create, read, update, and delete files.
- **Step 2**: In your **Main** method, create an instance of **FileManager** and a user interface that allows the user to choose a file and an operation (create, read, update, or delete), then calls the appropriate method on the **FileManager** instance.

Image Processing Tool

- **Step 1**: Choose an image processing library for C# (like System.Drawing or AForge.NET) and learn how to use it to open images and apply filters.
- **Step 2**: Create an **ImageProcessor** class with methods to apply different filters to an image.
- **Step 3**: In your **Main** method, create an instance of **ImageProcessor** and a user interface that allows the user to choose an image and a filter, then calls the appropriate method on the **ImageProcessor** instance and displays the resulting image.

Remember, these are just high-level guides. Each of these projects is quite complex and would require a lot more planning and coding to fully implement. But hopefully, these guides give you a good starting point.

These projects, along with the larger project of Developing an Inventory Management Web Application Using ASP.NET, will serve as a comprehensive showcase of your newfound skills and provide a sense of achievement as you demonstrate your abilities in real-world scenarios.

Building Use Case: Developing an MVC Web App using ASP.NET

We will delve into the exciting world of building a Model-View-Controller (MVC) web application using ASP.NET. MVC is a popular architectural pattern that separates the application into three interconnected components: the Model, View, and Controller. This pattern promotes modular, maintainable, and scalable code by keeping the concerns of data manipulation, user interface, and application logic separate.

let's walk through the process of building a basic MVC (Model-View-Controller) web application using ASP.NET Core.

Step 1: Set Up Your Development Environment

To write and run ASP.NET Core code, you need a development environment. If you don't have one set up yet, you can install Visual Studio, which is a popular IDE for C# development. You can download it from the official Microsoft website.

Step 2: Create a New ASP.NET Core Web Application

Once you have Visual Studio installed, open it and create a new ASP.NET Core Web Application project. Name it "MyFirstMvcApp".

Step 3: Choose the Web Application (Model-View-Controller) Template

In the "New ASP.NET Core Web Application" dialog, choose the "Web Application (Model-View-Controller)" template, which creates a project with a simple UI and support for MVC.

Step 4: Understand the Project Structure

The project you've created uses the MVC pattern, which stands for Model-View-Controller. This pattern divides your project into three interconnected parts:

- **Models**: Classes that represent the data of the app.
- **Views**: Files that display the app's user interface.
- **Controllers**: Classes that handle user input and interactions.

Step 5: Create a Model

Let's create a simple model. Right-click on the Models folder, select Add -> Class, name it "Person.cs", and add the following code:

```
public class Person
{
    public int Id { get; set; }
    public string Name { get; set; }
    public int Age { get; set; }
}
```

Step 6: Create a Controller

Next, we'll create a controller. Right-click on the Controllers folder, select Add -> Controller, choose "MVC Controller - Empty", and name it "PersonController". In the newly created **PersonController.cs**, add the following code:

```
public class PersonController : Controller
{
    public IActionResult Index()
    {
        var person = new Person { Id = 1, Name = "John Doe", Age = 30 };
        return View(person);
    }
}
```

Step 7: Create a View

Finally, we'll create a view. Right-click on the Views folder, select Add -> New Folder, and name it "Person". Then, right-click on the Person folder, select Add -> View, choose "Empty (without model)", and name it "Index". In the newly created **Index.cshtml**, add the following code:

```
@model MyFirstMvcApp.Models.Person


<h1>@Model.Name</h1>
<p>Age: @Model.Age</p>
```

Step 8: Run the Web Application

Press F5 or click the "Start Debugging" button to run the web application. Your default web browser should open and display the name and age of the person defined in the **PersonController**.

Try modifying the web application to add more features. For example, you could add a form to the person view that allows users to enter their own name and age, and then display this information back to them. The more you experiment and practice, the better you'll understand how to use ASP.NET Core to build MVC web applications.

Remember, this is a very basic example of what you can do with ASP.NET Core and MVC. As you become more comfortable with the framework, you can start building more complex web applications with multiple models, views, and controllers, as well as other features like user authentication and database access.

Chapter 5: Overcoming C# Challenges

Overview of Common Challenges Faced by C# Developers

As you progress in your C# programming journey, you will encounter various challenges that are unique to the language and its ecosystem.

Memory Management

One of the primary challenges in C# development is managing memory efficiently. C# is a managed language that uses automatic memory management through garbage collection. However, improper memory usage can lead to memory leaks and performance issues. To overcome this challenge, it is crucial to understand concepts like object lifetimes, disposal patterns, and using appropriate data structures to minimize memory overhead.

Performance Optimization

C# offers a high level of abstraction, but it also requires careful consideration of performance. Achieving optimal performance involves optimizing algorithms, minimizing unnecessary object allocations, and leveraging language features like async/await for efficient asynchronous programming. Profiling tools can help identify bottlenecks and guide performance improvements.

Exception Handling

Handling exceptions effectively is essential for writing robust and reliable C# code. Proper exception handling involves catching and handling exceptions at appropriate levels, logging exception details for debugging, and designing a structured exception hierarchy to provide meaningful error messages. Additionally, understanding exception propagation and using try-catch blocks judiciously is crucial for maintaining code integrity.

Concurrency and Multithreading

C# provides powerful tools and frameworks for concurrent and parallel programming. However, working with threads, tasks, and shared resources can introduce challenges like race conditions, deadlocks, and thread synchronization issues. To address these challenges, it is vital to have a solid understanding of synchronization primitives, thread-safe data structures, and best practices for multithreaded programming.

Dependency Management

In complex C# projects, managing dependencies and versioning can become challenging. It is important to use a robust package management system like NuGet and follow best practices for dependency injection to ensure seamless integration of libraries and frameworks. Understanding how to handle conflicting dependencies and upgrade packages effectively is crucial for maintaining a stable and up-to-date codebase.

Testing and Debugging

Testing and debugging are integral parts of the development process. Ensuring comprehensive test coverage and adopting practices like unit testing, integration testing, and automated testing can help catch bugs and ensure the reliability of your code. Additionally, leveraging debugging tools and techniques to diagnose and resolve issues efficiently is essential for smooth development.

Keeping Up with Evolving Technologies

The technology landscape is constantly evolving, and new frameworks, libraries, and features are introduced regularly in the C# ecosystem. Staying updated with the latest developments, attending conferences, participating in online communities, and continuously learning new techniques and frameworks will help you overcome the challenge of keeping up with the ever-changing technology landscape.

Strategies to Overcome These Challenges and Optimize C# Code

In the previous section, we discussed the common challenges faced by C# developers. Now, let's explore some effective strategies to overcome these challenges and optimize your C# code. By following these strategies, you can improve the performance, maintainability, and reliability of your applications.

Memory Management

To optimize memory usage in C#, consider the following strategies:

- Use object pooling: Instead of creating new objects frequently, reuse existing objects from a pool to minimize memory allocations and deallocations.

- Dispose of unmanaged resources: Implement the IDisposable interface and use the using statement to ensure timely disposal of unmanaged resources.

- Avoid unnecessary object cloning: Make use of references and shallow copying when appropriate to minimize memory overhead.

- Optimize large object allocations: For large objects, consider using memory-mapped files or memory-mapped streams to reduce memory pressure.

Performance Optimization

To improve the performance of your C# code, consider the following strategies:

- Use efficient data structures and algorithms: Choose the most suitable data structures and algorithms for your specific problem domain to optimize time complexity.

- Minimize unnecessary computations: Avoid redundant calculations by caching results, optimizing loops, and using lazy evaluation techniques.

- Leverage parallel processing: Utilize multi-threading and parallel programming techniques to distribute workloads and improve overall performance.

- Optimize I/O operations: Minimize disk reads and writes, optimize database queries, and use asynchronous programming techniques to avoid blocking operations.

Exception Handling

To handle exceptions effectively in C#, follow these strategies:

- Catch exceptions at the appropriate level: Catch exceptions where you can handle them effectively and provide meaningful error messages to users.

- Log exception details: Log exception information along with relevant context to aid in debugging and troubleshooting.

- Use custom exception types: Create custom exception classes to provide more specific information about different error scenarios.

- Handle expected exceptions: Identify and handle expected exceptions separately from unexpected exceptions to maintain program flow.

Concurrency and Multithreading

To address concurrency challenges in C#, consider the following strategies:

- Use thread synchronization mechanisms: Employ locks, mutexes, semaphores, and other synchronization primitives to prevent race conditions and ensure thread safety.

- Avoid unnecessary blocking: Use non-blocking synchronization techniques like concurrent collections, async/await patterns, and Task Parallel Library (TPL).

- Use thread-safe data structures: Choose thread-safe collections and implement proper synchronization mechanisms for shared resources.

- Design for scalability: Consider using message queues, event-driven architectures, and distributed systems to handle concurrent operations efficiently.

Dependency Management

To manage dependencies effectively in C#, consider these strategies:

- Use a package manager: Utilize a package manager like NuGet to manage and update external libraries and frameworks.

- Practice version control: Maintain a clear understanding of the versions and dependencies of the libraries you use.

- Employ dependency injection: Apply dependency injection patterns to decouple components and make them more testable and maintainable.

- Use modular design principles: Structure your codebase into cohesive modules to manage dependencies and improve code maintainability.

Testing and Debugging

To ensure the quality of your C# code, follow these strategies:

- Adopt a test-driven development approach: Write unit tests to verify the functionality of individual components and ensure code correctness.

- Utilize debugging tools: Familiarize yourself with debugging features and use them to identify and resolve issues efficiently.

- Perform code reviews: Engage in code reviews with colleagues or join open-source projects to receive feedback on your code and improve its quality.

- Continuously refactor and optimize: Regularly review and refactor your code to improve its design, maintainability, and performance.

As you progress in your C# journey, don't shy away from experimenting with different techniques, exploring best practices, and staying updated with the latest advancements in the C# ecosystem. The key to overcoming challenges and optimizing your C# code is continuous learning, practice, and a problem-solving mindset. Embrace the challenges as opportunities for growth and refinement, and you will become a skilled C# developer capable of building robust and high-performing applications.

Building Use Case: Optimizing C# Code Performance

Optimizing code performance is a crucial aspect of software development. Here's a step-by-step guide on how to optimize C# code performance:

Step 1: Understand the Problem

Before you start optimizing, you need to understand where the performance issues are coming from. Is your application running slow? Are certain operations taking longer than expected?

Step 2: Use Profiling Tools

Profiling tools can help you identify the parts of your code that are causing performance issues. Visual Studio includes a Performance Profiler that can analyze CPU usage, memory usage, and other performance metrics. Run your application with the Performance Profiler and look for any methods that are using a lot of CPU or memory.

Step 3: Optimize Your Code

Once you've identified the performance bottlenecks, you can start optimizing your code. Here are a few general tips for optimizing C# code:

- **Avoid unnecessary calculations**: If you're performing the same calculation multiple times, consider storing the result in a variable and reusing it.

- **Use the right data structures**: Different data structures have different performance characteristics. For example, if you're frequently searching for items, a **HashSet** or **Dictionary** might be more efficient than a **List**.

- **Minimize memory allocations**: Frequent memory allocations can cause performance issues due to the overhead of garbage collection. Try to reuse objects when possible, and consider using value types (structs) instead of reference types (classes) for small objects.

- **Use async/await for I/O operations**: If your application is spending a lot of time waiting for I/O operations (like network requests or file reads), consider using async/await to allow your application to do other work while waiting for the I/O operation to complete.

Step 4: Test Your Changes

After making changes, run your application with the Performance Profiler again to see if your changes have improved performance. Keep in mind that optimization can be a complex process, and it's possible that your changes might not have the desired effect, or might even make performance worse. If that's the case, don't be discouraged - just keep trying different approaches until you find one that works.

Step 5: Repeat

Performance optimization is often an iterative process. You might need to go through these steps multiple times, optimizing different parts of your code, until you're satisfied with your application's performance.

Remember, while it's important to write efficient code, it's also important not to prematurely optimize. Don't spend time optimizing parts of your code that aren't causing performance issues. As the saying goes, "Premature optimization is the root of all evil."

Book 3 - C# Programming: Advanced Concepts and Industry Practices

Introduction: Mastery in C#

The Importance of Advanced Topics in Professional C# Development

Embarking on the journey to become a proficient C# developer involves delving into a range of advanced topics. These concepts serve as the building blocks for creating robust, scalable, and high-quality applications. They not only refine your programming skills but also pave the way for exciting career opportunities, empowering you to tackle complex development challenges.

Staying abreast of the dynamic and evolving field of software development is crucial. Regular emergence of new technologies, frameworks, and best practices necessitates a continuous learning mindset. By immersing yourself in the depths of C#, you equip yourself with the skills to meet these industry demands, preparing you to handle cutting-edge projects and make meaningful contributions to the development community.

Efficiency and scalability become paramount as applications increase in complexity. The tools and techniques derived from a deeper understanding of C# allow for performance optimization, effective resource management, and scalable architecture design. This knowledge enables the development of high-performance applications that can handle large data volumes, meet growing user demands, and deliver a seamless user experience.

Emphasizing software engineering principles, design patterns, and best practices leads to clean, modular, and maintainable code. This results in improved code quality, simplified maintenance, and fosters better collaboration within development teams. Grasping principles such as SOLID, design patterns like the Factory Method or Observer, and architectural patterns like MVC or MVVM, contributes to creating well-structured and extensible codebases.

In a professional software development setting, effective collaboration and teamwork are key. A shared understanding of advanced C# concepts promotes this collaboration, allowing for confident communication of ideas, discussion of technical challenges, and meaningful contributions to team discussions on larger projects.

Intersection of C# with specialized domains and technologies opens new avenues of opportunity. For instance, web development concepts can lead to expertise in ASP.NET Core, web APIs, or front-end frameworks like React or Angular. Game development topics introduce frameworks like Unity or game physics libraries. Thus, a deeper exploration of C# can unlock potential in various specialized fields.

Preparing for Mastery Level in C#

Mastery in C# requires more than just a basic understanding of the language. It demands a profound comprehension of advanced concepts, adherence to industry practices, and a commitment to continuous learning. This path positions you as an expert C# developer, capable of handling intricate projects and making substantial contributions to the software development industry.

To prepare for C# mastery, it's crucial to broaden your knowledge beyond the fundamentals. This involves dedicating time to delve into advanced topics such as concurrency, memory management, asynchronous programming, design patterns, and performance optimization. Utilizing resources like books, online courses, tutorials, and industry blogs can deepen your understanding of these concepts, laying a strong foundation for advanced problem-solving and enabling you to develop efficient, scalable, and reliable applications.

As you progress, it's important to focus on mastering the language features and capabilities of C#. This includes familiarizing yourself with the latest updates and versions of the language and exploring advanced language features like LINQ, lambda expressions, delegates, events, and generics. Understanding these features allows you to write more concise, expressive, and efficient code. Implementing them in real-world scenarios can solidify your understanding and provide valuable hands-on experience.

Achieving C# mastery also involves embracing software engineering principles and best practices. Developing a deep understanding of SOLID principles, design patterns, clean code practices, and test-driven development provides a solid framework for writing maintainable, extensible, and well-structured code. Applying these principles to your projects not only enhances the quality of your code but also promotes collaboration and maintainability.

Broadening your expertise also involves exploring popular frameworks and libraries within the C# ecosystem. Familiarizing yourself with frameworks such as ASP.NET Core, Entity

Framework, Xamarin, and WPF allows you to leverage their power to build robust and feature-rich applications. Experimenting with different frameworks and libraries can provide hands-on experience and expand your toolkit.

A critical aspect of preparing for C# mastery is building real-world applications. Undertaking challenging projects that push your boundaries and require the application of advanced concepts and industry practices can provide invaluable experience. Engaging in open-source projects or creating your own projects to solve complex problems exposes you to different scenarios and helps you understand the nuances of software development in a practical setting.

Finally, attaining mastery in C# requires adopting a mindset of continuous learning. Staying updated with the latest trends, advancements, and best practices in the industry is crucial. Engaging with the developer community through forums, meetups, and online communities allows for knowledge exchange, shared experiences, and collaboration with like-minded professionals. Embracing feedback and seeking opportunities for mentorship and guidance can accelerate your learning and growth.

Chapter 1: Advanced C# Constructs: Delegates, Events, and LINQ

Deep Dive into Delegates and Events in C#

We will explore advanced C# constructs that are fundamental to developing robust and flexible applications: delegates, events, and LINQ. Delegates and events provide powerful mechanisms for handling callbacks and event-driven programming, while LINQ (Language Integrated Query) enables efficient data querying and manipulation. Understanding and mastering these constructs will significantly enhance your ability to design and implement complex solutions in C#.

Delegates

A delegate in C# is a type that represents references to methods with a particular parameter list and return type. When you instantiate a delegate, you can associate its instance with any method that matches its signature. Delegates are used to pass methods as arguments to other methods.

Here's an example of a delegate:

```
public delegate int MyDelegate(int x, int y);


public class Program
{
    public static int Add(int a, int b)
    {
        return a + b;
    }
}
```

```
public static void Main()

{

    MyDelegate del = Add;

    int result = del(10, 20);

    Console.WriteLine(result);  // Outputs: 30

    }

}
```

In this example, **MyDelegate** is a delegate that can point to methods that take two integers as parameters and return an integer. The **Add** method matches this signature, so we can create an instance of **MyDelegate** that points to **Add**.

Events

Events in C# are a way for a class to provide notifications to clients of that class when some interesting thing happens to an object. The most familiar use for events is in graphical user interfaces; typically, the classes that represent controls in the interface have events that are notified when the user does something to the control (for example, click a button).

Events are a special kind of multicast delegate that can only be invoked from within the class or struct where they are declared (the publisher class). If other classes or structs subscribe to the event, their event handler methods will be called when the publisher class raises the event.

Here's an example of an event:

```
public class Publisher

{

    public event EventHandler MyEvent;


    public void RaiseEvent()

    {

        MyEvent?.Invoke(this, EventArgs.Empty);

    }

}
```

```
public class Subscriber
{
    public void OnMyEvent(object sender, EventArgs e)
    {
        Console.WriteLine("Event raised!");
    }
}


public class Program
{
    public static void Main()
    {
        Publisher pub = new Publisher();
        Subscriber sub = new Subscriber();

        pub.MyEvent += sub.OnMyEvent;

        pub.RaiseEvent(); // Outputs: "Event raised!"
    }
}
```

In this example, **Publisher** is a class that declares an event called **MyEvent**. **Subscriber** is a class that declares a method **OnMyEvent** that matches the signature of the **EventHandler** delegate. In the **Main** method, we subscribe **OnMyEvent** to **MyEvent**, so when **MyEvent** is raised (by calling **RaiseEvent**), **OnMyEvent** is called.

Introduction to Language Integrated Query (LINQ)

Language Integrated Query (LINQ) is a powerful feature in C# that allows you to work with data in a more intuitive and flexible way. It introduces standard, easily-learned patterns for querying and updating data, and the technology can be extended to support potentially any kind of data store.

LINQ is integrated into C# (and VB .NET) and is similar in syntax to SQL, making it more straightforward to query data inside your applications. It can be used to query, in a type-safe way, any collection of objects, databases, XML, and more.

Here are the main types of LINQ:

- **LINQ to Objects**: This allows you to query any collection implementing **IEnumerable\<T\>**, like arrays or lists.

- **LINQ to SQL**: Also known as DLINQ, it allows you to query relational databases.

- **LINQ to XML**: Also known as XLINQ, it provides a in-memory XML programming interface.

- **LINQ to Entities**: This is a part of ADO.NET Entity Framework, and allows you to query relational databases.

Here's an example of how you might use LINQ to Objects to filter a list of integers:

```
List<int> numbers = new List<int> { 1, 2, 3, 4, 5, 6, 7, 8, 9, 10 };


IEnumerable<int> evenNumbers = from num in numbers
                where num % 2 == 0
                select num;


foreach (int num in evenNumbers)
{
    Console.WriteLine(num);
}
```

In this example, we're using LINQ to select only the even numbers from the list. The **from num in numbers** is similar to the **FROM** clause in SQL, specifying the data source. The **where num % 2 == 0** is like the **WHERE** clause in SQL, specifying the filter to apply. Finally, **select num** specifies what we want to select from the data source, similar to the **SELECT** clause in SQL.

The result of this LINQ query is an **IEnumerable<int>** that contains only the even numbers from the list. We then print these numbers to the console.

Building Use Case: Building a Command-Line Application

let's build a simple command-line application that uses delegates, events, and LINQ. We'll create an application that manages a list of students and allows the user to add students and display all students with a grade above a certain threshold.

Step 1: Define the Student Class

First, we'll define a **Student** class that represents a student with a name and a grade:

```
public class Student
{
    public string Name { get; set; }
    public int Grade { get; set; }
}
```

Step 2: Define the StudentManager Class

Next, we'll define a **StudentManager** class that manages a list of students. This class will have an **AddStudent** method to add a student to the list, and a **StudentsAboveGrade** method to get all students with a grade above a certain threshold using LINQ:

```
public class StudentManager
{
    private List<Student> students = new List<Student>();

    public void AddStudent(Student student)
    {
        students.Add(student);
    }
```

```csharp
public IEnumerable<Student> StudentsAboveGrade(int grade)

    {

        return students.Where(s => s.Grade > grade);

    }

}
```

Step 3: Define the Event and Delegate

We'll define an event in the **StudentManager** class that gets triggered when a student is added. We'll also define a delegate that represents the event handler methods for this event:

```csharp
public delegate void StudentAddedEventHandler(Student student);


public class StudentManager

{

    public event StudentAddedEventHandler StudentAdded;


    // ... rest of the class ...


    public void AddStudent(Student student)

    {

        students.Add(student);

        StudentAdded?.Invoke(student);

    }

}
```

Step 4: Handle the Event

In the **Main** method, we'll subscribe to the **StudentAdded** event and print a message to the console whenever a student is added:

```csharp
public static void Main()

{

    StudentManager manager = new StudentManager();
```

```
manager.StudentAdded += student =>
{
    Console.WriteLine($"Added student: {student.Name}");
};


// ... rest of the Main method ...
}
```

Step 5: Implement the User Interface

Finally, we'll implement a simple command-line user interface that allows the user to add students and display all students with a grade above a certain threshold:

```
public static void Main()
{
    // ... event subscription ...

    while (true)
    {
        Console.WriteLine("Enter command (add/display/quit):");
        string command = Console.ReadLine();

        if (command == "add")
        {
            Console.WriteLine("Enter student name:");
            string name = Console.ReadLine();

            Console.WriteLine("Enter student grade:");
            int grade = int.Parse(Console.ReadLine());

            manager.AddStudent(new Student { Name = name, Grade = grade });
```

```csharp
    }
    else if (command == "display")
    {
        Console.WriteLine("Enter grade threshold:");
        int grade = int.Parse(Console.ReadLine());


        IEnumerable<Student> students = manager.StudentsAboveGrade(grade);


        foreach (Student student in students)
        {
            Console.WriteLine($"{student.Name}: {student.Grade}");
        }
    }
    else if (command == "quit")
    {
        break;
    }
  }
}
```

In this user interface, the user can enter "add" to add a student, "display" to display all students with a grade above a certain threshold, or "quit" to exit the application. When a student is added, the **StudentAdded** event is triggered, and a message is printed to the console.

Chapter 2: C# in Web Design and Component-Based Programming

Exploring Frameworks for Web Design in C#

As the demand for dynamic and user-friendly web experiences continues to grow, it becomes crucial for developers to leverage the power of C# in web design. By understanding and utilizing frameworks specifically designed for web development, developers can create scalable and efficient web applications that meet industry standards.

Frameworks for Web Design in C#

1. ASP.NET: ASP.NET is a mature and widely adopted web application framework developed by Microsoft. It provides a powerful set of tools, libraries, and components for building dynamic websites, web services, and web applications. ASP.NET enables developers to use C# for server-side scripting, allowing them to create responsive and feature-rich web experiences. It offers various features like model-view-controller (MVC) architecture, built-in security mechanisms, and seamless integration with databases.

2. ASP.NET Core: ASP.NET Core is the next generation of ASP.NET, designed to be cross-platform and highly modular. It provides a lightweight and flexible framework for developing web applications using C#. ASP.NET Core offers improved performance, scalability, and support for cloud-based deployment. With its modular architecture and support for dependency injection, developers have greater flexibility in choosing the components and libraries they need for their web projects.

3. Blazor: Blazor is a framework that allows developers to build interactive web user interfaces using C# and HTML. It enables the creation of Single Page Applications (SPAs) where the user interface is rendered on the client-side using WebAssembly or

server-side using SignalR. Blazor provides a familiar programming model for C# developers, allowing them to leverage their existing skills to create dynamic web applications. With Blazor, developers can write both the client-side and server-side logic in C#, resulting in a streamlined development process.

4. Xamarin: While primarily known for mobile app development, Xamarin can also be used for creating web applications using C#. Xamarin.Forms, a UI toolkit, enables developers to build cross-platform web applications that run on multiple devices and platforms. By sharing a significant portion of the codebase, developers can save time and effort in developing web applications for different platforms.

Understanding the MVC (Model-View-Controller) Pattern and Its Applications

The MVC pattern is a widely used architectural pattern that separates the concerns of data management, user interface presentation, and application logic. Understanding the MVC pattern is crucial for building scalable, maintainable, and testable web applications in C#. By following this pattern, developers can achieve better code organization, improved reusability, and enhanced development efficiency.

The MVC Pattern

The MVC pattern consists of three core components: the Model, the View, and the Controller. Each component has its own responsibility and interacts with the others in a coordinated manner.

1. Model: The Model represents the data and business logic of the application. It encapsulates the data structures, operations, and rules that govern the application's behavior. In C#, the Model can be implemented using classes, structs, or other data structures. It handles data storage, retrieval, and manipulation, ensuring the integrity and consistency of the application's data.

2. View: The View is responsible for presenting the application's user interface to the end-user. It displays the data from the Model and provides a means for user interaction. In

C#, Views are typically implemented using HTML, CSS, and client-side scripting languages like JavaScript. Views are designed to be visually appealing and user-friendly, enabling users to interact with the application's data and functionality.

3. Controller: The Controller acts as an intermediary between the Model and the View. It receives user input from the View, processes it, and updates the Model accordingly. The Controller coordinates the flow of data and controls the application's behavior. In C#, Controllers are implemented as classes that handle user requests, perform business logic operations, and update the Model or select appropriate Views to display.

Applications of the MVC Pattern in C# Web Design

The MVC pattern is widely used in C# web design frameworks like ASP.NET MVC and ASP.NET Core MVC. These frameworks provide a structured approach to building web applications, leveraging the MVC pattern to achieve separation of concerns and maintainable codebases. By adopting the MVC pattern, developers can create flexible and scalable web applications that can be easily maintained and extended.

Component Structures, JavaScript Nesting, and Iteration Mechanisms

We will explore the component structures, JavaScript nesting, and iteration mechanisms used in C# web design and component-based programming. These concepts are essential for building dynamic and interactive web applications using C#. Understanding how components are structured, how JavaScript nesting works, and how to iterate over data efficiently is key to creating robust and efficient web experiences.

Component Structures

Component-based programming is a popular approach in web development, allowing developers to break down the user interface into reusable and independent components. Components are self-contained elements with their own logic and user interface. They can be combined to create complex web applications.

In C#, various frameworks like Blazor and ASP.NET Core provide component-based architectures. Components are typically structured using a combination of HTML, CSS, and C#

code. The HTML portion defines the layout and structure of the component, while the C# code handles the logic and data management. By organizing the application into components, developers can achieve code reusability, modularity, and maintainability.

JavaScript Nesting

JavaScript is often used in conjunction with C# to enhance the interactivity and functionality of web applications. Nesting JavaScript code within C# components allows for dynamic manipulation of the user interface based on user actions or data changes.

JavaScript nesting involves embedding JavaScript code within the HTML or Razor syntax of a component. This enables developers to manipulate the DOM (Document Object Model) and respond to user events. By combining the power of C# and JavaScript, developers can create rich and interactive web experiences.

Iteration Mechanisms

Iterating over data is a common task in web development, especially when working with dynamic content or collections. C# provides various iteration mechanisms that allow developers to loop through data efficiently.

One common iteration mechanism is the foreach loop, which simplifies the process of iterating over collections such as arrays or lists. This loop automatically iterates over each element of the collection without the need to manage indices or boundaries manually.

Another useful iteration mechanism in C# is LINQ (Language Integrated Query). LINQ provides a powerful and expressive way to query and manipulate data. With LINQ, developers can perform complex filtering, sorting, and transformation operations on data collections using a declarative syntax.

By leveraging these iteration mechanisms, developers can efficiently process and manipulate data in web applications, enhancing performance and productivity.

Building Use Case: Developing a Single-Page Web Application

Creating a single-page web application (SPA) in C# typically involves using ASP.NET Core for the backend and a JavaScript framework like Angular, React, or Vue.js for the frontend.

However, with the introduction of Blazor, you can now build interactive web UIs using C# instead of JavaScript. In this guide, we'll use Blazor to build a simple SPA.

Step 1: Install the Necessary Tools

First, you'll need to install .NET Core SDK and Visual Studio. You can download them from the official Microsoft website.

Step 2: Create a New Blazor WebAssembly Project

Open Visual Studio and create a new project. Select "Blazor App" and click "Next". Enter a name for the project and click "Create". On the next screen, select "Blazor WebAssembly App" and click "Create".

Step 3: Understand the Project Structure

A new Blazor project includes several files and folders:

- **wwwroot**: This folder contains static files, such as HTML, CSS, and JavaScript files.
- **Pages**: This folder contains the components that represent pages in the application.
- **Shared**: This folder contains components that can be shared across multiple pages.
- **App.razor**: This file is the main entry point for the application.
- **Program.cs**: This file sets up the application's startup configuration.

Step 4: Create a New Page

In the **Pages** folder, create a new file called **MyPage.razor**. In this file, you can define a new page for the application:

```
@page "/mypage"
```

```
<h1>Welcome to My Page!</h1>
```

```
<p>This is a new page in the application.</p>
```

The **@page** directive at the top specifies the route for this page.

Step 5: Add A Link to The New Page

Open the **Shared/NavMenu.razor** file. This file defines the navigation menu for the application. Add a new list item for your page:

```
<li class="nav-item px-3">
    <NavLink class="nav-link" href="mypage">
        <span class="oi oi-list-rich" aria-hidden="true"></span> My Page
    </NavLink>
</li>
```

Step 6: Run the Application

You can now run the application by pressing F5 or clicking the "Start Debugging" button. The application will open in a new browser window. You should see the "My Page" link in the navigation menu, and clicking this link will take you to your new page.

Step 7: Add Interactivity

Blazor allows you to add interactivity to your pages using C#. For example, you can add a button that increments a counter:

```
@page "/mypage"

<h1>Welcome to My Page!</h1>

<p>Counter: @counter</p>

<button class="btn btn-primary" @onclick="IncrementCounter">Increment</button>

@code {
    private int counter;

    void IncrementCounter()
    {
```

```
        counter++;

    }

}
```

In this code, **@counter** is a field that holds the current counter value. **@onclick** is an event that is triggered when the button is clicked, and **IncrementCounter** is a method that increments the counter.

This is a very basic example of a SPA in Blazor. A real-world application would likely involve more complex components, services for data access, and perhaps integration with an API for server-side operations.

Chapter 3: Responsive Design and Device Usability

The Importance of Device-Responsive Development (PC, Mobile, Smartphone)

In today's digital age, where users access websites and applications from various devices such as PCs, laptops, tablets, and smartphones, it is crucial for developers to prioritize device-responsive development. Device responsiveness ensures that the user interface and user experience of an application adapt seamlessly to different screen sizes, resolutions, and orientations. This chapter explores the importance of device-responsive development in the context of C# and highlights the significance of providing a consistent and optimized experience across different devices.

The Significance of Device-Responsive Development

1. Enhanced User Experience: Device-responsive development enables users to access and interact with applications seamlessly across different devices. By optimizing the layout, content, and functionality for each screen size, users can have an intuitive and engaging experience regardless of the device they use. Responsive design eliminates the need for users to zoom in or scroll horizontally, improving overall usability.

2. Increased Reach and Accessibility: With the increasing usage of mobile devices, ensuring a responsive design allows applications to reach a wider audience. By catering to the unique requirements of mobile users, developers can tap into a larger market and provide a seamless experience for users on the go. Responsive design also promotes accessibility, ensuring that individuals with disabilities can access and navigate applications effectively.

3. Improved Performance and Speed: Responsive design goes hand in hand with optimizing the performance and speed of an application. By tailoring the content and assets to specific devices, developers can reduce unnecessary data transfer, enhance loading times,

and minimize bandwidth usage. This results in faster and more efficient user experiences, reducing bounce rates and improving user satisfaction.

4. Consistent Branding and Design: Device-responsive development enables the consistent presentation of branding, aesthetics, and design elements across different devices. Maintaining a unified brand experience enhances brand recognition and trust among users. By adapting the layout and visual elements to fit different screen sizes, developers can ensure a cohesive and recognizable brand image.

5. Future-Proofing Applications: With the constant evolution of technology and the introduction of new devices, device-responsive development future-proofs applications. By adopting responsive design principles and techniques, developers can adapt to emerging devices and technologies without the need for major redevelopment or redesign. This flexibility ensures that applications remain relevant and accessible in a rapidly changing digital landscape.

Introduction to Razor Pages and Telerik for Improving Usability

In the realm of web development, creating responsive and user-friendly interfaces is essential to provide a positive user experience. Razor Pages and Telerik.

Understanding Razor Pages

Razor Pages is a feature of ASP.NET Core that simplifies the development of web pages by combining HTML and C# code within a single file. This approach enables developers to create dynamic and interactive web pages with ease. Razor Pages provide an intuitive way to handle user interactions, manage data, and perform server-side operations. By leveraging the Razor Pages framework, developers can enhance the usability of their applications by providing a seamless and responsive user interface.

Benefits of Razor Pages:

1. Simplified Development: With Razor Pages, developers can build web pages quickly and efficiently by combining HTML markup and C# code. The simplicity and familiarity of the Razor syntax make it easier to create dynamic and interactive elements, reducing development time and effort.

2. Improved Maintainability: Razor Pages promote a clean and modular code structure. By encapsulating the logic of each page within a single file, it becomes easier to maintain and update the application. The separation of concerns allows developers to focus on specific functionality within individual Razor Pages.

3. Enhanced User Experience: Razor Pages enable the creation of dynamic and responsive web interfaces. Developers can use Razor syntax to customize content based on user interactions and display real-time data. This capability enhances the overall user experience by providing a more interactive and personalized interface.

Introduction to Telerik

Telerik is a comprehensive suite of UI controls and components for building web applications. It offers a wide range of pre-built UI elements, such as grids, charts, calendars, and form controls, that can be seamlessly integrated into C# projects. Telerik simplifies the implementation of advanced user interface features and provides a consistent and visually appealing design across different devices and platforms.

Benefits of Telerik:

1. Rich User Interface: Telerik provides a collection of professionally designed UI components that enhance the visual appeal and usability of web applications. The extensive library of controls offers advanced features and interactivity, enabling developers to create engaging and intuitive user interfaces.

2. Cross-Platform Compatibility: Telerik is designed to work seamlessly across different devices and platforms, ensuring a consistent experience for users. The components are responsive and adapt to various screen sizes, enabling developers to build applications that are accessible and functional on both desktop and mobile devices.

3. Time-Saving and Productivity: Telerik accelerates development by providing ready-to-use components and controls that can be easily integrated into C# projects. This eliminates the need for developers to create custom UI elements from scratch, saving time and effort. The intuitive API and documentation further enhance productivity and enable developers to quickly implement complex features.

Building Use Case: Creating a Responsive Web Page with Razor Pages

Creating a responsive web page with Razor Pages in ASP.NET Core involves a few steps. In this guide, we'll create a simple responsive web page that displays well on both desktop and mobile devices.

Step 1: Install the Necessary Tools

First, you'll need to install .NET Core SDK and Visual Studio. You can download them from the official Microsoft website.

Step 2: Create a new Razor Pages project

Open Visual Studio and create a new project. Select "Razor Pages" and click "Next". Enter a name for the project and click "Create".

Step 3: Understand the Project Structure

A new Razor Pages project includes several files and folders:

- **wwwroot**: This folder contains static files, such as HTML, CSS, and JavaScript files.
- **Pages**: This folder contains the Razor Pages of the application.
- **Startup.cs**: This file sets up the application's startup configuration.

Step 4: Add Bootstrap for Responsiveness

ASP.NET Core Razor Pages projects come with Bootstrap, a popular CSS framework for building responsive websites. You can find the Bootstrap CSS file in **wwwroot/lib/bootstrap/dist/css**.

Step 5: Create a new Razor Page

In the **Pages** folder, right-click and select "Add" -> "Razor Page". Enter a name for the page and click "Add". This will create a new **.cshtml** file for the page.

Step 6: Design the Page Layout using Bootstrap

In the **.cshtml** file, you can use Bootstrap classes to design a responsive layout. For example:

```
<div class="container">

  <div class="row">

    <div class="col-md-8">

      <h1>Welcome to My Page!</h1>

      <p>This is a responsive web page.</p>

    </div>

    <div class="col-md-4">

      <h2>About</h2>

      <p>This page is built with Razor Pages and Bootstrap.</p>

    </div>

  </div>

</div>
```

In this example, the **container** class provides a centered container for the page content, the **row** class creates a new row, and the **col-md-8** and **col-md-4** classes create two columns that stack vertically on medium and smaller devices and display side by side on larger devices.

Step 7: Run the Application

You can now run the application by pressing F5 or clicking the "Start Debugging" button. The application will open in a new browser window. You should see your new page, and if you resize the browser window, you'll see that the layout adjusts for different screen sizes.

Chapter 4: C# in Software Engineering

Application of C# in Software Engineering Projects

We delve into the practical application of C# in software engineering projects. C# is a versatile programming language that offers a wide range of capabilities for developing robust and scalable software solutions. In this chapter, we explore how C# is utilized in various stages of software engineering, including requirements analysis, design, implementation, testing, and maintenance.

C# in Requirements Analysis

During the requirements analysis phase, software engineers gather and document the functional and non-functional requirements of a software project. C# can be used to develop prototypes or proof-of-concept applications to demonstrate specific functionalities or validate requirements. With its extensive libraries and frameworks, C# enables engineers to quickly develop prototypes and gather feedback from stakeholders.

C# in Software Design

In the software design phase, engineers translate the requirements into a well-structured design that outlines the system's architecture, modules, and interfaces. C# provides powerful object-oriented programming (OOP) features that allow engineers to design and implement reusable and maintainable code. By leveraging concepts such as classes, inheritance, and interfaces, C# enables engineers to create modular and extensible software designs.

C# in Implementation

The implementation phase involves writing code based on the software design. C# offers a rich set of features and libraries that simplify the implementation process. From built-in data types to advanced language constructs, C# provides a solid foundation for writing efficient and expressive code. Additionally, the vast array of available frameworks and libraries in the C# ecosystem allows engineers to leverage pre-built solutions and accelerate development.

C# in Testing

Testing is a crucial aspect of software engineering to ensure the quality and reliability of the software. C# offers various testing frameworks, such as NUnit and MSTest, which provide tools for unit testing, integration testing, and automated testing. These frameworks, coupled with C#'s support for test-driven development (TDD), enable engineers to write comprehensive test suites and automate the testing process for efficient and reliable software testing.

C# in Maintenance

Software maintenance involves making modifications, fixing bugs, and adding new features to the existing software. C#'s readable and maintainable code structure makes it easier for engineers to understand and modify the codebase. The language's support for encapsulation, inheritance, and polymorphism facilitates code reuse and extensibility, reducing the effort required for maintenance tasks.

Application of C# in Software Engineering Projects

1. Desktop Applications: C# is widely used for developing desktop applications using frameworks like Windows Presentation Foundation (WPF) and Windows Forms. These frameworks provide rich user interfaces and seamless integration with the Windows operating system, making C# a popular choice for building feature-rich and user-friendly desktop applications.

2. Web Development: C# is extensively used in web development with frameworks like ASP.NET and ASP.NET Core. These frameworks enable engineers to build scalable and secure web applications, leveraging C#'s strong typing, powerful libraries, and support for web standards. C# can be used for server-side programming, handling requests, managing data, and implementing business logic.

3. Mobile App Development: With frameworks like Xamarin, C# can be used to develop cross-platform mobile applications for iOS, Android, and Windows. Xamarin allows engineers to write code once and deploy it across multiple platforms, saving development

time and effort. C# offers access to native device functionalities and seamless integration with platform-specific APIs, providing a native-like experience for mobile app users.

4. Cloud Computing: C# is well-suited for cloud computing and can be used with platforms like Microsoft Azure to develop scalable and cloud-native applications. Azure provides various services and tools that integrate seamlessly with C#, enabling engineers to build distributed and highly available applications that leverage the power of the cloud.

The application of C# in software engineering projects is vast and encompasses various stages of the software development lifecycle. From requirements analysis to implementation, testing, and maintenance, C# provides a robust and flexible platform for building reliable and scalable software solutions. Whether it's desktop applications, web development, mobile apps, or cloud computing, C# empowers engineers to deliver high-quality software that meets the demands of today's industry.

Understanding Design Patterns and Architecture in C#

Design patterns provide proven solutions to common software design problems, while architecture defines the overall structure and organization of a software system. Understanding and applying design patterns and architecture principles in C# can significantly enhance the quality, maintainability, and scalability of software projects.

Design Patterns

Design patterns are typical solutions to common problems in software design. Each pattern is like a blueprint that you can customize to solve a particular design problem in your code. They are categorized into three groups: Creational, Structural, and Behavioral.

1. **Creational Patterns**: These patterns deal with object creation mechanisms, trying to create objects in a manner suitable to the situation. Examples include Singleton, Factory Method, and Abstract Factory.

2. **Structural Patterns**: These patterns deal with object composition, or, how the entities can use each other. Examples include Adapter, Decorator, and Composite.

3. **Behavioral Patterns**: These patterns are concerned with communication between objects. Examples include Observer, Strategy, and Template Method.

Software Architecture

Software architecture is about making fundamental structural choices that are costly to change once implemented. It provides an abstraction to manage the system complexity and establish a communication and coordination mechanism among components.

1. **MVC (Model-View-Controller)**: This pattern separates an application into three main components: the model, the view, and the controller. The ASP.NET MVC framework is a popular choice for building web applications using this pattern.

2. **MVVM (Model-View-ViewModel)**: This pattern is commonly used in WPF, Xamarin, and UWP applications. It separates the UI (View) from the data (Model) with the help of ViewModel.

3. **Layered Architecture**: This pattern separates concerns into layers such as Presentation Layer, Business Layer, and Data Access Layer, which can be a good choice for enterprise applications.

4. **Microservices Architecture**: This architectural style structures an application as a collection of loosely coupled services. Each service is a small, independent unit that performs a single operation.

Key Design Patterns in C#

1. Singleton Pattern: The Singleton pattern ensures that a class has only one instance and provides global access to it. It is useful when a single instance of a class needs to be shared across the application, such as a logger or a configuration manager.

2. Factory Pattern: The Factory pattern provides an interface for creating objects without specifying their concrete classes. It enables developers to delegate the object creation process to a separate class, improving code flexibility and decoupling.

3. Observer Pattern: The Observer pattern establishes a one-to-many relationship between objects, allowing changes in one object to be automatically reflected in other dependent objects. This pattern is commonly used in event-driven systems and GUI frameworks.

4. Decorator Pattern: The Decorator pattern allows adding additional functionality to an object dynamically. It enables developers to extend the behavior of an object without modifying its original implementation. This pattern is useful for achieving flexible and modular code.

Benefits of Design Patterns and Architecture in C#

1. Code Reusability: Design patterns promote the reuse of proven solutions, reducing the need to reinvent the wheel for common problems.

2. Maintainability: Well-designed software architecture and the use of design patterns improve code organization and modularity, making it easier to maintain and enhance the system over time.

3. Scalability: Architecture patterns like microservices enable applications to scale horizontally by adding or removing independent services as needed.

4. Flexibility: By separating concerns and applying design patterns, C# applications become more flexible and adaptable to changing requirements.

Building Use Case: Developing a WPF Application

let's create a simple WPF (Windows Presentation Foundation) application using C#. We'll create a simple application that allows users to enter their name and then displays a greeting message when they click a button.

Step 1: Install the Necessary Tools

First, you'll need to install .NET Core SDK and Visual Studio. You can download them from the official Microsoft website.

Step 2: Create a new WPF App project

Open Visual Studio and create a new project. Select "WPF App (.NET Core)" and click "Next". Enter a name for the project and click "Create".

Step 3: Understand the Project Structure

A new WPF project includes several files and folders:

*   **App.xaml**: This file defines the startup URI (the first window to open when the application starts) and any application-wide resources.

*   **MainWindow.xaml**: This file defines the main window of the application.

*   **MainWindow.xaml.cs**: This file contains the code-behind for the main window.

Step 4: Design the User Interface

Open **MainWindow.xaml**. In this file, you can define the user interface of the main window using XAML. For our application, we'll add a **TextBox** for the user to enter their name, a **Button** to display the greeting, and a **Label** to display the greeting:

```xml
<Window x:Class="WpfApp.MainWindow"
    xmlns="http://schemas.microsoft.com/winfx/2006/xaml/presentation"
    xmlns:x="http://schemas.microsoft.com/winfx/2006/xaml"
    Title="Greeting App" Height="200" Width="400">
  <StackPanel Margin="10">
    <TextBox x:Name="NameTextBox" PlaceholderText="Enter your name" />
    <Button x:Name="GreetButton" Content="Greet" Click="GreetButton_Click" Margin="0,10,0,0" />
    <Label x:Name="GreetingLabel" />
  </StackPanel>
</Window>
```

Step 5: Add Interactivity

Open **MainWindow.xaml.cs**. In this file, you can add code to handle events, such as button clicks. For our application, we'll add code to display a greeting when the button is clicked:

```csharp
public partial class MainWindow : Window
{
  public MainWindow()
  {
    InitializeComponent();
  }

  private void GreetButton_Click(object sender, RoutedEventArgs e)
  {
    string name = NameTextBox.Text;
    GreetingLabel.Content = $"Hello, {name}!";
  }
}
```

157

}

You can now run the application by pressing F5 or clicking the "Start Debugging" button. The application will open in a new window. You should be able to enter your name, click the "Greet" button, and see a greeting message.

Chapter 5: Testing and Debugging in C#

Importance of Testing in C# Development

Testing is an essential part of the software development lifecycle, as it ensures the functionality, reliability, and quality of the application. By thoroughly testing C# code, developers can identify and fix bugs, validate the behavior of their programs, and ensure that their software meets the required specifications. Effective testing and debugging practices play a vital role in building robust and error-free applications.

The Importance of Testing in C# Development

1. Bug Detection and Prevention: Testing helps detect and prevent bugs in the code. By executing various test cases and scenarios, developers can identify any unexpected behavior or defects in the software. Early bug detection enables prompt bug fixing, reducing the likelihood of issues arising in production.

2. Quality Assurance: Testing ensures that the application meets the desired quality standards. It verifies that the software functions as intended, performs the expected operations, and produces accurate results. Thorough testing improves the reliability and usability of the application.

3. Increased Stability: Rigorous testing enhances the stability of the software. By uncovering and addressing potential issues early on, developers can improve the overall performance and resilience of the application. This leads to a more stable and reliable user experience.

4. User Satisfaction: Testing plays a significant role in ensuring customer satisfaction. A thoroughly tested application is less likely to have critical issues or unexpected behaviors, providing users with a smooth and consistent experience. High-quality software builds trust and fosters positive user engagement.

5. Reduced Maintenance Costs: Identifying and resolving bugs during the development phase is more cost-effective than addressing them in the production environment. Testing helps catch errors early, reducing the effort and cost required for maintenance and support later on.

6. Compliance and Industry Standards: Many industries have strict regulatory requirements and standards. Proper testing ensures that the application adheres to these guidelines, ensuring compliance and reducing legal and financial risks.

Testing Strategies in C# Development

1. Unit Testing: Unit testing involves testing individual units or components of code in isolation. By writing test cases for specific methods or functions, developers can verify that each unit behaves as expected. Unit testing frameworks like NUnit or MSTest provide tools to automate and streamline this process.

2. Integration Testing: Integration testing focuses on verifying the interaction between different components or modules of the software. It ensures that the integrated system functions correctly and that the components work together seamlessly.

3. System Testing: System testing evaluates the overall behavior and functionality of the complete system. It tests the application as a whole, considering various scenarios and user interactions. System testing verifies that the software meets the specified requirements and performs reliably.

4. Performance Testing: Performance testing assesses the responsiveness, scalability, and efficiency of the application under different load conditions. It helps identify bottlenecks, memory leaks, and other performance-related issues.

5. Regression Testing: Regression testing ensures that changes or updates to the codebase do not introduce new defects or impact existing functionality. It involves rerunning previously executed test cases to validate that the system behaves consistently after modifications.

Debugging in C# Development

In addition to testing, effective debugging is crucial for identifying and resolving issues in the code. Debugging tools in C#, such as breakpoints, watch windows, and stepping through code, help developers trace the execution flow and identify the root causes of errors. By carefully analyzing the code and its behavior during runtime, developers can locate and fix bugs more efficiently.

Testing and debugging are essential components of the C# development process. By placing a strong emphasis on testing, developers can ensure that their software functions as intended, meets quality standards, and provides a positive user experience. Thorough testing helps detect and prevent bugs, enhances stability, reduces maintenance costs, and ensures compliance with industry standards

Strategies and Tools for Effective Debugging in C#

Debugging is the process of identifying and resolving issues or bugs in the code to ensure the software functions as intended. Effective debugging is essential for improving code quality, identifying root causes of errors, and enhancing overall software reliability.

Strategies for Effective Debugging in C#

1. Reproducing the Issue: The first step in debugging is to reproduce the problem consistently. This involves identifying the specific inputs, conditions, or scenarios that trigger the issue. By replicating the problem, developers can gain insights into its causes and better understand the context in which it occurs.

2. Analyzing Error Messages and Stack Traces: Error messages and stack traces provide valuable information about the location and nature of the problem. By carefully examining these messages, developers can narrow down the scope of the issue and identify the relevant portions of the code where the problem might reside.

3. Utilizing Breakpoints: Breakpoints allow developers to pause the execution of the program at specific lines of code. This enables them to inspect variables, evaluate expressions, and step through the code to understand its flow. By strategically placing breakpoints, developers can pinpoint the exact point of failure and examine the state of the program during runtime.

4. Logging and Tracing: Logging statements and tracing techniques can help capture valuable information about the program's execution. By adding logging statements at critical points in the code, developers can gather insights into the flow of the program and

track the values of variables or method invocations. This can assist in identifying patterns, inconsistencies, or unexpected behaviors that may contribute to the bug.

5. Debugging Tools: C# provides a range of powerful debugging tools that aid in the debugging process. Integrated Development Environments (IDEs) like Visual Studio offer features such as watch windows, immediate windows, and call stack navigation, which allow developers to examine variables, inspect object properties, and trace the execution flow. These tools provide a comprehensive debugging environment to diagnose and resolve issues effectively.

6. Binary Search: In complex scenarios, where the cause of the bug is difficult to identify, developers can utilize a binary search approach. By selectively enabling or disabling portions of the code, developers can narrow down the problematic section and isolate the root cause more efficiently.

7. Collaboration and Code Reviews: Debugging is not solely an individual effort. Collaborating with peers and conducting code reviews can provide fresh perspectives and insights into the problem. By discussing the issue with others, developers can gain new ideas and approaches to address the bug.

Effective debugging is crucial for ensuring high-quality software development in C#. By employing strategies such as reproducing the issue, analyzing error messages, utilizing breakpoints, logging, and leveraging debugging tools, developers can efficiently diagnose and resolve bugs.

Building Use Case: Implementing a Test Suite for a C# Project

Creating a test suite for a C# project typically involves using a testing framework like MSTest, NUnit, or xUnit. In this guide, we'll use MSTest, which is built into Visual Studio.

Step 1: Install Tools

First, you'll need to install .NET Core SDK and Visual Studio. You can download them from the official Microsoft website.

Step 2: Create a new MSTest Test Project

Open Visual Studio and create a new project. Select "MSTest Test Project (.NET Core)" and click "Next". Enter a name for the project and click "Create".

Step 3: Project Structure

A new MSTest project includes several files:

- **UnitTest1.cs**: This file contains a sample unit test. You can rename this file and add your own tests to it.

- **.csproj**: This file contains information about the project and its dependencies.

Step 4: Write a test

Open **UnitTest1.cs**. In this file, you can write your tests. Each test is a method marked with the **[TestMethod]** attribute. For example, let's write a test that checks if the addition of two numbers is correct:

```
[TestClass]
public class UnitTest1
{
    [TestMethod]
    public void TestAddition()
    {
        int a = 2;
        int b = 3;
        int sum = a + b;
        Assert.AreEqual(5, sum);
    }
}
```

In this example, **Assert.AreEqual** checks if the two arguments are equal. If they're not, the test fails.

Step 5: Run the tests

You can run the tests by opening the Test Explorer (go to "Test" > "Test Explorer" in the menu) and clicking "Run All". You should see your test in the list, and if the test passes, it will be marked with a green checkmark.

Step 6: Add more tests

You can add more tests by adding more methods with the **[TestMethod]** attribute. Ideally, you should have at least one test for each method in your application. You can also organize tests into different classes or even different projects.

Step 7: Run the tests again

After adding more tests, you can run them all again by clicking "Run All" in the Test Explorer.

Chapter 6: Professional C# Projects

Advanced Projects that Demonstrate Professional C# Development

These projects are designed to provide you with hands-on experience and practical examples of real-world C# development scenarios. By working on these projects, developers can solidify their understanding, enhance their skills, and gain valuable insights into professional C# development practices.

Project 1: Building a Chat Application

1. **Setup:** Start by setting up an ASP.NET Core project. You'll also need to add SignalR and Entity Framework Core to your project.

2. **User Management:** Use ASP.NET Core Identity to implement user registration and login.

3. **Real-Time Communication:** Use SignalR to enable real-time communication between the server and the clients. You'll need to create a SignalR hub that manages connections and handles incoming messages.

4. **Data Storage:** Use Entity Framework Core to store chat messages and user data in a database. You'll need to create models for your data and set up database context.

5. **Frontend:** Create views for user registration, login, and chat rooms. You'll also need to write JavaScript code to handle real-time communication on the client side.

Project 2: Developing a Data Analytics Dashboard

1. **Setup:** Start by setting up an ASP.NET Core project. You'll also need to add Entity Framework Core to your project.

2. **Data Access:** Use Entity Framework Core to access your data. This might involve setting up models and database context, and writing queries to retrieve the data you need for your dashboard.

3. **Data Processing:** Depending on your data, you might need to perform some processing on the server side before sending it to the client. This could involve calculations, aggregations, or transformations.

4. **Data Visualization:** Use a JavaScript library like D3.js or Chart.js to create interactive visualizations of your data. This will involve writing JavaScript code that fetches data from your server and uses it to generate charts or graphs.

Project 3: Building a Recommendation Engine

1. **Setup:** Start by setting up an ASP.NET Core project. You'll also need to add ML.NET to your project.

2. **Data Access:** Use Entity Framework Core to access your data. This might involve setting up models and database context, and writing queries to retrieve the data you need for your recommendation engine.

3. **Machine Learning:** Use ML.NET to train a recommendation model on your data. This will involve choosing an appropriate algorithm, setting up a pipeline, and training the model.

4. **Recommendations:** Once your model is trained, you can use it to generate recommendations. This might involve writing a method that takes a user's history as input and returns a list of recommended items.

Project 4: Creating an E-commerce Platform

1. **Setup:** Start by setting up an ASP.NET Core project. You'll also need to add Entity Framework Core to your project.

2. **User Management:** Use ASP.NET Core Identity to implement user registration and login.

3. **Product Catalog:** Create models for your products and use Entity Framework Core to store them in a database. You'll need to create views for displaying the product catalog, individual product details, and search results.

4. **Shopping Cart:** Implement a shopping cart where users can add products, view their cart, and proceed to checkout.

5. **Order Processing:** Implement order processing, including collecting shipping information, calculating totals, and handling payment.

Project 5: Building a Content Management System (CMS)

1. **Setup:** Start by setting up an ASP.NET Core project. You'll also need to add Entity Framework Core to your project.

2. **User Management:** Use ASP.NET Core Identity to implement user registration and login.

3. **Content Management:** Implement functionality for creating, editing, and publishing content. This might involve creating models for your content, setting up views for content creation and editing, and implementing a workflow for content approval and publishing.

4. **Roles and Permissions:** Implement roles and permissions to control who can do what in your CMS. This might involve creating roles, assigning roles to users, and checking permissions when performing actions.

Remember, these are complex projects that will take time and effort to complete. Don't rush, take your time to understand each step, and don't hesitate to look up tutorials or ask for help if you get stuck. Good luck!

Hands-on Experience with Full-Cycle C# Project Development

Gaining hands-on experience with full-cycle C# project development involves going through all the stages of software development, from requirements gathering to deployment and maintenance. Here's a step-by-step guide using a hypothetical project - let's say we're building a web-based task management application.

1. **Requirements Gathering:** Discuss with stakeholders to understand what they want from the application. For our task management application, we might need features like creating tasks, assigning tasks to users, tracking task progress, and so on.

1. **Design:** Plan out how the application will work. This might involve creating wireframes for the user interface, designing the database schema, and deciding on the architecture of the application (like whether to use MVC, MVVM, etc.).

2. **Development:** Start coding the application. In C#, this might involve setting up an ASP.NET Core project for the web application, creating models for the tasks and users, setting up controllers to handle web requests, and creating views for the user interface.

5. **Testing:** Write tests for your code to make sure it works as expected. This might involve unit tests (to test individual methods), integration tests (to test how different parts of the application work together), and end-to-end tests (to test the application as a whole).

6. **Deployment:** Once the application is working and tested, it's time to deploy it. This might involve setting up a server, installing the .NET runtime, and deploying the application files. If you're using a cloud provider like Azure, it might also involve setting up a CI/CD pipeline to automate the deployment process.

7. **Maintenance:** After the application is deployed, it will need to be maintained. This might involve fixing bugs, adding new features, and periodically updating the application to use the latest versions of .NET and other dependencies.

8. **Documentation:** Throughout the project, it's important to document your work. This might involve writing comments in your code, documenting how to use the application, and writing technical documentation for other developers.

Building Use Case: Developing a Unity Game

Creating a Unity game involves a wide range of tasks, and the specifics can vary greatly depending on the type of game you're making. However, I'll provide a step-by-step guide to creating a basic 2D platformer game in Unity using C#.

Step 1: Install Unity and Visual Studio
Download and install Unity and Visual Studio from their respective official websites.

Step 2: Create a new Unity project
Open Unity Hub and create a new 2D project.

Step 3: Import or create assets

For a basic game, you'll need a few assets such as sprites for characters and environments. You can create these yourself or find them online. Once you have your assets, import them into Unity.

Step 4: Create the game environment

Use the imported assets to create your game environment. This could include platforms, obstacles, background elements, etc.

Step 5: Create the player character

In the Unity editor, go to the Hierarchy window and click on the "+" button. From the dropdown menu, select **2D Object > Sprite**. This will create a new sprite game object in your scene.

In the Inspector window, you'll see a field labeled **Sprite** under the **Sprite Renderer** component. Click on the small circle next to this field to open the Select Sprite window. From here, you can select a sprite that you've imported into your project. If you haven't imported any sprites yet, you can do so by dragging and dropping image files into the Project window.

With the player sprite selected, go to the Inspector window and click on the **Add Component** button. In the search bar that appears, type "Rigidbody2D" and select it from the dropdown menu. This will add a Rigidbody2D component to your sprite.

The Rigidbody2D component allows your sprite to be affected by 2D physics. For example, you can apply forces to the sprite to move it around, and it will automatically react to collisions with other objects.

Still with the player sprite selected, go back to the Inspector window and click on the **Add Component** button again. This time, type "BoxCollider2D" in the search bar and select it from the dropdown menu. This will add a BoxCollider2D component to your sprite.

The BoxCollider2D component allows your sprite to detect collisions with other objects. By default, the BoxCollider2D will automatically size itself to fit your sprite, but you can adjust its size and position if needed.

At this point, you should have a player character that can move around and interact with the physics engine. You can control its movement by applying forces to the Rigidbody2D component, and you can detect when it collides with other objects by using the BoxCollider2D component.

Step 6: Write a player movement script

Create a new C# script for controlling the player's movement. This script should handle input from the player (e.g., arrow keys or WASD keys for movement, spacebar for jumping) and move the character accordingly.

Here's a basic example of what the player movement script might look like:

```csharp
using System.Collections;

using System.Collections.Generic;

using UnityEngine;


public class PlayerMovement : MonoBehaviour
{
    public float moveSpeed = 5f;
    public float jumpForce = 5f;
    private bool isJumping = false;
    private Rigidbody2D rb;


    void Start()
    {
        rb = GetComponent<Rigidbody2D>();
    }


    void Update()
    {
        float moveX = Input.GetAxis("Horizontal");


        rb.velocity = new Vector2(moveX * moveSpeed, rb.velocity.y);
```

```
if (Input.GetButtonDown("Jump") && !isJumping)
    {
        rb.AddForce(new Vector2(0f, jumpForce), ForceMode2D.Impulse);
        isJumping = true;
    }
}


void OnCollisionEnter2D(Collision2D collision)
{
    if (collision.gameObject.CompareTag("Ground"))
    {
        isJumping = false;
    }
}
}
```

This script allows the player to move left or right based on the horizontal input and jump when the Jump button (usually the spacebar) is pressed.

Step 7: Attach the script to the player character

Back in Unity, select the player character in the Hierarchy panel. In the Inspector panel, click "Add Component" > "Scripts" and select the "PlayerMovement" script. This will attach the script to the player character.

Step 8: Test the game

Click the "Play" button at the top of the Unity interface. You should be able to move the player character around the screen using the arrow keys or WASD keys and make the character jump using the spacebar.

This is a very basic example of a Unity game. A real-world game would likely involve more complex gameplay, multiple scenes, animations, sound effects, and much more. But this should give you a good starting point for developing games in Unity using C#.

Chapter 7: Mastering the Final Project

Walkthrough of the Building Use Case: Deploying a C# Application to Azure

This chapter provides a comprehensive walkthrough of the building use case, guiding readers through the process of deploying their C# application to the Azure cloud platform. By mastering this final project, readers will gain valuable experience in leveraging the power of Azure for hosting and scaling their applications.

Deploying a C# application to Azure involves several steps. Here's a step-by-step guide on how to do it:

Step 1: Create an Azure Account

If you don't have an Azure account, you'll need to create one. You can sign up for a free account on the Azure website.

Step 2: Install Azure CLI

Azure CLI is a command-line tool that you can use to manage Azure resources. You can download it from the Azure website.

Step 3: Create a Web App in Azure

You can create a new Web App in Azure using the Azure portal or the Azure CLI. Here's how to do it using the Azure CLI:

1. Open a command prompt or terminal.
2. Log in to Azure by running the command **az login**. This will open a browser window where you can log in to your Azure account.

3. Once you're logged in, create a new resource group by running the command **az group create --name myResourceGroup --location "West Europe"**. Replace "myResourceGroup" with the name you want to use for your resource group, and "West Europe" with the location you want to use.

4. Create a new Web App by running the command **az webapp create --resource-group myResourceGroup --plan myAppServicePlan --name myWebApp --runtime "DOTNET|5.0" --deployment-local-git**. Replace "myResourceGroup" with the name of your resource group, "myAppServicePlan" with the name you want to use for your App Service plan, and "myWebApp" with the name you want to use for your Web App.

Step 4: Deploy Your Application

You can deploy your application to Azure using Git. Here's how to do it:

1. In your application's directory, initialize a new Git repository by running the command **git init**.

2. Add all your files to the repository by running the command **git add ..**

3. Commit your files by running the command **git commit -m "Initial commit"**.

4. Add a remote for your Azure Web App by running the command **git remote add azure <git clone url>**. Replace "<git clone url>" with the Git clone URL of your Azure Web App. You can find this URL in the Azure portal, in the Overview section of your Web App.

5. Push your application to Azure by running the command **git push azure master**.

Your application should now be deployed to Azure. You can access it by navigating to **https://<app-name>.azurewebsites.net**, replacing "<app-name>" with the name of your Web App.

Remember to replace all placeholders with your actual values. Also, ensure that your application is configured to listen on the port provided by the **WEBSITE_PORT** environment variable, as this is the port that Azure will use to serve your application.

Building a Robust Enterprise Software Solution Using C#, WPF, and Azure

Building a robust enterprise software solution involves a lot of steps and code, and it's beyond the scope of this platform to provide a complete, detailed guide with all the code. However, I can provide a high-level guide with some example code snippets to give you an idea of how you might approach such a project.

Step 1: Requirements Gathering

Before you start coding, you need to understand what you're building. This might involve meetings with stakeholders, creating mockups, and writing a detailed specification.

Step 2: Setting Up the Development Environment

Install Visual Studio and the Azure SDK. Create a new WPF project in Visual Studio.

Step 3: Developing the WPF Application

Start by creating the main window of your application. In WPF, the UI is usually defined using XAML. Here's an example of what the XAML for your main window might look like:

```
<Window x:Class="MyApp.MainWindow"
    xmlns="http://schemas.microsoft.com/winfx/2006/xaml/presentation"
    xmlns:x="http://schemas.microsoft.com/winfx/2006/xaml"
    Title="My App" Height="450" Width="800">
  <Grid>
    <!-- Your UI elements go here -->
  </Grid>
</Window>
```

Step 4: Setting Up Azure Services

In the Azure portal, create a new SQL Database. This will involve choosing a subscription, resource group, database name, server, and pricing tier.

Step 5: Connecting to the Azure SQL Database

In your WPF application, you can use the System.Data.SqlClient namespace to connect to your Azure SQL Database. Here's an example of how you might do this:

```
string connectionString = "Server=tcp:myserver.database.windows.net,1433;Initial Catalog=mydatabase;Persist
Security Info=False;User
ID=myusername;Password=mypassword;MultipleActiveResultSets=False;Encrypt=True;TrustServerCertificate=
False;Connection Timeout=30;";
using (SqlConnection connection = new SqlConnection(connectionString))
{
    connection.Open();
    // Execute commands against the database here
}
```

Step 6: Implementing Functionality

Implement the functionality of your application. This will involve writing a lot of C# code and XAML. The specifics will depend on what your application needs to do.

Step 7: Testing

Test your application thoroughly. This might involve writing unit tests, performing manual testing, or even setting up automated UI tests.

Step 8: Deployment

Deploy your WPF application to your users. This might involve publishing it to a shared network drive, distributing it via an installer, or even publishing it to the Microsoft Store.

Deploy your Azure services. This will involve clicking the "Publish" button in the Azure portal.

Remember, this is a high-level guide and each step can involve a lot of work. Building a robust enterprise software solution is a big project, but it's also a great way to learn about software development and improve your C# programming skills.

Strategies and Best Practices for Project Completion and Optimization

Strategies and Best Practices:

1. Project Planning and Management: Successful project completion starts with effective planning and management. This phase involves defining project goals, creating a project plan, setting milestones, and establishing a timeline. It is crucial to allocate resources, assign tasks, and communicate effectively with the development team. Regular project monitoring and adapting to changes are also key aspects of project management.

2. Code Review and Refactoring: To optimize the C# application, developers should conduct thorough code reviews. This practice helps identify potential issues, code smells, and areas for improvement. By refactoring the code, developers can enhance readability, maintainability, and performance. It involves optimizing algorithms, eliminating redundant code, and applying best coding practices to ensure clean and efficient code.

3. Performance Optimization: Performance is a critical factor in software development. This phase focuses on identifying and addressing performance bottlenecks in the C# application. Techniques such as code profiling, identifying resource-intensive operations, and optimizing database queries can significantly improve the application's speed and responsiveness. Additionally, caching mechanisms, asynchronous programming, and efficient memory management should be employed to enhance performance.

4. Error Handling and Exception Management: Robust error handling and exception management are crucial for producing high-quality software. This phase involves implementing effective error handling mechanisms, including logging, exception handling, and graceful error recovery. Developers should strive to provide meaningful error messages to aid troubleshooting and debugging.

5. Security and Data Protection: Security is a critical consideration in any software project. This phase focuses on implementing robust security measures to protect sensitive data and prevent unauthorized access. It includes employing secure authentication and

authorization mechanisms, encrypting data at rest and in transit, and following security best practices to mitigate potential vulnerabilities.

6. Testing and Quality Assurance: Thorough testing and quality assurance are essential to ensure the reliability and functionality of the C# application. This phase involves writing comprehensive test cases, conducting unit testing, integration testing, and system testing. Additionally, developers should consider implementing automated testing frameworks and continuous integration practices to streamline the testing process and improve overall software quality.

7. Documentation and User Support: Proper documentation and user support are crucial for project completion. This phase involves creating clear and comprehensive documentation that includes user manuals, API documentation, and code documentation. It also includes providing user support channels, such as online forums, knowledge bases, and timely responses to user queries.

Book 4 - C++ Programming: A Practical Introduction

Introduction: Diving into C++

Introduction to C++ and its Role in the Programming World

As one of the most widely used programming languages, C++ offers a powerful and versatile platform for developing a wide range of applications, from system software to games, embedded systems, and high-performance applications.

C++ has a rich history and has been a popular choice for software development since its inception in the late 1970s. It is an extension of the C programming language, incorporating additional features and capabilities that enable developers to write efficient and complex programs. C++ is known for its flexibility, performance, and ability to handle low-level programming tasks while also supporting high-level abstractions.

C++ is an object-oriented programming language that provides a comprehensive set of features for developing robust and efficient applications. It combines procedural, object-oriented, and generic programming paradigms, allowing developers to organize code into reusable modules, create complex data structures, and utilize powerful abstractions.

One of the key features of C++ is its ability to directly access memory locations and interact with hardware. This low-level control makes it suitable for developing systems-level software, such as operating systems, device drivers, and embedded systems. At the same time, C++ offers higher-level abstractions, including classes, templates, and polymorphism, enabling developers to write code that is both efficient and maintainable.

Role of C++ in the Programming World

C++ has a wide range of applications and is used in various industries. Some of the key areas where C++ excels include:

1. **System Programming:** C++ is extensively used for developing system software, such as operating systems, device drivers, and embedded systems. Its ability to work at a low level and directly manipulate hardware makes it a preferred choice for such applications.

2. **Game Development:** Many popular games, including AAA titles, are developed using C++. The language provides the performance and control necessary for building complex and resource-intensive game engines.

3. **High-Performance Computing:** C++ is widely used in fields such as scientific research, finance, and engineering, where high-performance computing is crucial. Its ability to efficiently handle complex algorithms and utilize hardware resources makes it suitable for such applications.

4. **Networking and Communications:** C++ is commonly used in networking and communication protocols, where efficiency and reliability are essential. It allows developers to create efficient networked applications, such as routers, servers, and communication middleware.

5. **Cross-Platform Development:** C++ is a portable language, allowing developers to write code that can be compiled and executed on different platforms. This cross-platform capability makes it a preferred choice for developing applications that need to run on multiple operating systems.

Installing Necessary Tools to Start C++ Programming

Before diving into C++ programming, it is essential to set up the development environment and ensure that we have the required tools and resources to write, compile, and run C++ code effectively.

Setting Up the Development Environment

To begin our journey into C++, we need to set up the development environment, which typically involves the following steps:

Choose a C++ Compiler

A C++ compiler is a software tool that translates C++ source code into executable machine code. There are several C++ compilers available, both open-source and commercial. Some popular options include GCC (GNU Compiler Collection), Clang, and Microsoft Visual C++. Choose the compiler that best suits your needs and install it on your system.

Integrated Development Environment (IDE)

An IDE provides a comprehensive development environment with features such as code editing, debugging, and project management. It streamlines the development process and enhances productivity. Some widely used C++ IDEs include Visual Studio, Code::Blocks, and Eclipse. Install an IDE that aligns with your preferences and requirements.

Installation Steps

Follow the installation instructions provided by your chosen compiler and IDE. Download the installation package from the official website or use a package manager if available. Pay attention to any additional dependencies or configurations required during the installation process.

Verify the Installation

Once the installation is complete, verify that the tools are properly installed. Open your IDE and create a new C++ project or file. Write a simple "Hello, World!" program and compile it. Execute the compiled program to ensure that everything is functioning correctly. This step confirms that the compiler, IDE, and associated tools are set up correctly.

Online IDEs and Platforms

Alternatively, if you prefer a web-based development environment or do not want to install software on your local machine, there are online IDEs and platforms available. These platforms provide an integrated online coding environment, eliminating the need for local installations. Examples of online platforms for C++ programming include Replit, CodeSandbox, and JDoodle. Simply create an account on the platform of your choice and start coding within your web browser.

By installing the necessary tools such as a C++ compiler and an IDE, developers can create a robust foundation for their C++ projects. Whether you choose a local installation or prefer online platforms, ensuring that the tools are properly configured and functional is essential before diving into the world of C++ programming. With a properly set up development environment, we are now ready to explore the language further and delve into the core concepts and practical applications of C++.

Chapter 1: C++ Fundamentals

Understanding the Basics of C++ Programming

Understanding these fundamental concepts is crucial for building a strong foundation in C++ development. We will explore the key elements of the language, syntax, and programming constructs that form the building blocks of C++ programs.

Here are some of the basic concepts in C++ programming:

1. **Variables and Data Types**: In C++, you need to specify the type of variable you're declaring. The basic types include integers (int), floating-point numbers (float), characters (char), and booleans (bool).

2. **Control Structures**: These include if-else statements, switch-case, and loops (for, while, do-while). They are used to perform different actions based on different conditions.

3. **Functions**: Functions are blocks of code that perform specific tasks. A C++ program has at least one function, which is main(), and all the most trivial programs can define additional functions.

4. **Arrays and Strings**: An array is used to store multiple variables of the same type. A string is an array of characters.

5. **Pointers**: A pointer is a variable that stores the memory address of another variable. Pointers are a powerful feature of the C++ language, but they can also lead to errors if not used properly.

6. **Classes and Objects**: C++ is an object-oriented programming language. This means that it uses classes to organize code around objects. A class defines the data and behavior of an object.

7. **Inheritance and Polymorphism**: These are key features of object-oriented programming. Inheritance allows a class to inherit the properties and methods of another class. Polymorphism allows a child class to provide a different implementation of a method that is already provided by its parent class.

8. **Standard Template Library (STL)**: The STL is a library in C++ that provides several generic classes and functions, including collections and algorithms, which can be very useful for reducing the amount of code you have to write.

9. **Exception Handling**: C++ provides a mechanism to handle exceptions, which are runtime errors. This mechanism uses the try, catch, and throw keywords.

10. **File I/O**: C++ supports input and output operations with files through a simple and flexible set of classes.

Learning C++ can be challenging but rewarding. It's a powerful language that's used in a wide range of applications, from game development to software engineering. It's also a great language to learn if you're interested in understanding more about how computers work at a lower level.

Explanation of the Structure of a Basic C++ Program

A C++ program is composed of various elements that work together to perform a task. Understanding the structure of a basic C++ program is essential for anyone learning the language. This article will delve into the fundamental components of a C++ program, including preprocessor directives, the main function, statements, expressions, and comments.

Preprocessor Directives

The first line of a typical C++ program often begins with a preprocessor directive. Preprocessor directives are lines included in the code of programs that are not program statements but directives for the preprocessor. These lines are always preceded by a hash sign (#). The preprocessor processes these directives before the actual compilation of code begins.

The most common preprocessor directive is **#include**, which is used to include the contents of another file in the current file at the point of inclusion. For instance, **#include <iostream>** tells the preprocessor to include the iostream standard file. This file is essential because it allows for input and output in a C++ program. Without it, you wouldn't be able to use **cin** to receive input or **cout** to output information.

The Main Function

Every C++ program must have a main function. The operating system runs the main function whenever a program is executed. The main function serves as the starting point of every C++ program. It is usually written as **int main()**. The **int** before **main** signifies that the main function will return an integer. The pair of parentheses () can hold parameters, although they are empty in the case of **main**.

The body of the main function is enclosed in braces {}. All the executable code must be placed inside these braces. The main function typically returns a value, which is indicated by the **return 0;** statement. This statement signifies that the program has executed successfully.

Statements and Expressions

Inside the main function, we write various statements and expressions, which are the instructions that tell the computer what to do. Each statement in C++ ends with a semicolon (;). An expression is a combination of variables, constants, and operators written according to the syntax of C++. For example, **int a = 10;** is a statement, and **a + 10** is an expression.

Comments

Comments are used to explain the code and improve its readability. They are not executed by the compiler and do not affect the output of the program. In C++, single-line comments are created using **//**, and multi-line comments are created by enclosing the comment in **/*** and ***/**.

Here is a simple example of a C++ program:

```
// This is a simple C++ program
#include <iostream>

int main() {
    // Print a message to the screen
    std::cout << "Hello, World!" << std::endl;
    return 0;
}
```

In this program, the **#include <iostream>** line is a preprocessor directive that includes the iostream standard file. This file allows us to use the **std::cout** object to output information.

The **int main**() line is the beginning of the main function. This function will always be the starting point of our programs.

The **std::cout << "Hello, World!" << std::endl;** line is a statement that prints "Hello, World!" to the screen. The **std::endl** part of this line is used to insert a new line.

Finally, the **return 0;** line signifies that the program has finished executing successfully.

Chapter 2: C++ Operations

Deep Dive into Operators and Their Use in C++

Operators in C++ are symbols that instruct the compiler to perform specific mathematical or logical manipulations. They are used to manipulate data and variables and form the backbone of any computational instruction set in a program.

C++ has a rich set of operators, which can be broadly classified into the following categories: Arithmetic, Relational, Logical, Bitwise, Assignment, and Miscellaneous operators.

Arithmetic operators are used to perform common mathematical operations like addition, subtraction, multiplication, and division. For instance, in the expression **a + b**, **+** is the arithmetic operator, and **a** and **b** are operands. The modulus operator **%** is also an arithmetic operator used to find the remainder of a division operation.

Relational operators are used to compare two values and determine the relationship between them. These operators include **==** (equal to), **!=** (not equal to), **>** (greater than), **<** (less than), **>=** (greater than or equal to), and **<=** (less than or equal to). The result of a relational operation is a boolean value, either true or false.

Logical operators are used to combine the results of two or more conditions. The logical AND operator **&&** returns true if both conditions are true. The logical OR operator **||** returns true if at least one condition is true. The logical NOT operator **!** inverts the truth value of the operand.

Bitwise operators operate on binary representations of integers. They include bitwise AND **&**, bitwise OR **|**, bitwise XOR **^**, bitwise NOT **~**, left shift **<<**, and right shift **>>**. These operators are often used in low-level programming, such as device drivers, low-level graphics, cryptography, and optimization of program code.

Assignment operators are used to assign values to variables. The basic assignment operator is **=**, but there are also compound assignment operators like **+=**, **-=**, ***=**, **/=**, and **%=** that perform an operation and assignment in one step.

Miscellaneous operators include the size of operator, comma operator, ternary operator, and others. The size of operator **sizeof** is used to get the size of a variable or data type. The comma operator **,** is used to link related expressions together. The ternary operator **?:** is a shorthand way of writing an if-else statement.

Understanding and using operators effectively is crucial in C++ programming. They allow you to control the flow of a program and manipulate data in complex ways. With a solid grasp of operators, you can write more efficient and readable code.

Understanding Various Data Operations in C++

Arithmetic Operations

Arithmetic operations involve performing mathematical calculations on numeric data types. C++ provides a range of arithmetic operators, including addition (+), subtraction (-), multiplication (*), division (/), and modulus (%). These operators allow us to perform basic arithmetic calculations on variables and constants.

For example:

int a = 10;

int b = 5;

int sum = a + b;   // Addition

int difference = a - b;   // Subtraction

*int product = a * b;   // Multiplication*

int quotient = a / b;   // Division

int remainder = a % b;   // Modulus

Assignment Operations

Assignment operations are used to assign values to variables. The assignment operator (=) is used to store a value in a variable. It is essential to understand the difference between the assignment operator and the equality operator (==). The assignment operator assigns a value, while the equality operator compares two values for equality.

For example:

int x = 5;   // Assigning the value 5 to variable x

Comparison Operations

Comparison operations are used to compare two values and evaluate their relationship. C++ provides comparison operators such as equal to (==), not equal to (!=), greater than (>), less than (<), greater than or equal to (>=), and less than or equal to (<=). These operators return a boolean value (true or false) based on the comparison result.

For example:

int x = 5;

int y = 3;

bool isEqual = (x == y);   // Is x equal to y? (false)

bool isGreater = (x > y);   // Is x greater than y? (true)

Logical Operations

Logical operations involve combining and evaluating logical expressions. C++ provides logical operators such as logical AND (&&), logical OR (||), and logical NOT (!). These operators are used to create conditional expressions and control the flow of execution based on certain conditions.

For example:

bool condition1 = true;

bool condition2 = false;

bool result1 = condition1 && condition2;   // Logical AND (false)

bool result2 = condition1 || condition2;   // Logical OR (true)

bool result3 = !condition1;   // Logical NOT (false)

Bitwise Operations

Bitwise operations are used to manipulate individual bits of data. They are commonly used in low-level programming and for working with binary data. C++ provides bitwise operators such as bitwise AND (&), bitwise OR (|), bitwise XOR (^), bitwise complement (~), left shift (<<), and right shift (>>).

For example:

```
unsigned int a = 5;   // Binary representation: 0101
unsigned int b = 3;   // Binary representation: 0011
unsigned int result1 = a & b;   // Bitwise AND: 0001 (1)
unsigned int result2 = a | b;   // Bitwise OR: 0111 (7)
unsigned int result3 = a ^ b;   // Bitwise XOR: 0110 (6)
```

Chapter 3: Introduction to Pointers and Handlers in C++

Explanation of Pointers, Their Uses, and Their Importance in C++

Pointers are a fundamental part of C++, and understanding them is crucial to becoming proficient in the language. A pointer is a variable that holds the memory address of another variable. This allows for powerful and flexible programming techniques, such as dynamic memory allocation, data structures like trees and linked lists, and function arguments passed by reference.

What are Pointers?

A pointer is a variable, just like any other variable you might define, but instead of holding a direct value, it holds a memory address. This memory address is the location of another variable in memory.

You can declare a pointer with the ***** operator. For example, **int* p;** declares a pointer to an integer. You can assign it the address of another variable with the address-of operator **&**. For example, **int x = 10; int* p = &x;** makes **p** point to **x**.

Dereferencing Pointers

The act of accessing the value stored in the location a pointer is pointing to is called dereferencing. The dereference operator ***** is used to access this value. For example, if **p** is a pointer to **x**, ***p** will give you the value of **x**.

Uses of Pointers

1. **Dynamic Memory Allocation**: Pointers are used to allocate memory dynamically on the heap. This memory doesn't get cleared up automatically, and you can control its lifetime. Functions like **malloc()**, **calloc()**, **realloc()**, and **free()** are used in C for dynamic memory allocation. In C++, **new** and **delete** are used.

2. **Data Structures**: Pointers are used to create complex data structures like linked lists, trees, and graphs. For example, in a linked list, each node contains data and a pointer to the next node.

3. **Passing Function Arguments by Reference**: In C++, pointers can be used to pass arguments to a function by reference. This means that the function doesn't operate on a copy of the data, but on the original data itself. This can make your program more memory-efficient and can also allow a function to modify the values of the arguments.

4. **Pointers to Functions**: In C++, you can have pointers to functions. This means you can pass functions as arguments to other functions, return them from functions, and store them in data structures.

Importance of Pointers

Pointers provide a way to use the memory efficiently, manipulate data in complex ways, and increase the performance of the program. They are essential for dynamic memory allocation, where the efficient use of memory can drastically improve the performance of large-scale systems. Moreover, pointers form the basis of several data structures and allow for the creation of complex algorithms. Without pointers, data structures like linked lists, trees, and graphs would not be possible.

Explanation of Handlers and Their Role in C++ Programming

In C++, the term "handler" is often used in the context of exception handling, where it refers to a block of code that responds to a specific type of exception. Exception handling is a mechanism that handles runtime anomalies or exceptional conditions, allowing the flow of the program to change based on exceptions that occur during the execution of the program.

What are Exception Handlers?

An exception handler in C++ is code that is defined in a **catch** block. When an exception is thrown using the **throw** keyword, the flow of control stops and moves to the nearest matching catch block, if one exists. If no matching catch block is found, the program terminates.

Here's a basic example of an exception handler:

```
try {
    // Code that could throw an exception
    throw std::runtime_error("A problem occurred");
}
catch (const std::runtime_error& e) {
    // This is the handler for exceptions of type std::runtime_error
    std::cerr << "Caught exception: " << e.what() << '\n';
}
```

In this example, the **catch** block is the exception handler. It specifies that it will catch exceptions of type **std::runtime_error** (or any type derived from **std::runtime_error**). The handler code then outputs an error message.

Role of Handlers in C++ Programming

Exception handlers play a crucial role in robust and resilient C++ programming:

- **Error Handling**: The primary role of handlers is to manage errors or exceptional situations that arise during the execution of a program. This could include runtime errors, logic errors, or system-generated errors.

- **Resource Management**: Handlers often include cleanup code to free resources that were in use when an exception occurred. This could include dynamically allocated memory, file handles, network connections, etc.

- **Program Recovery**: By catching exceptions, a handler can allow a program to recover from an error, rather than crashing or exiting unexpectedly. The handler might include code to correct the issue, or it might allow the program to continue running in a degraded state.

- **Error Propagation**: If a function detects an error but isn't equipped to handle it, it can throw an exception. The exception will propagate up the call stack to a function that includes a suitable handler.

Chapter 4: Low-Level Programming with C++

Understanding Low-Level Programming and Its Relation to Operating Services

Low-level programming involves working at a level closer to the hardware and operating system, where we have direct control over memory, CPU registers, and system resources. Understanding low-level programming is essential for tasks such as device driver development, operating system development, and optimizing performance-critical code.

What is Low-Level Programming?

Low-level programming refers to writing code that interacts directly with hardware and system-level components. Unlike high-level programming languages, which provide abstractions and hide the low-level details, low-level programming requires a deep understanding of the underlying hardware architecture, memory management, and system services.

Relationship to Operating Services

Low-level programming is closely tied to operating services due to the following reasons:

- System Access: Low-level programming allows developers to access and control various operating system services and resources. This includes managing memory, interacting with hardware devices, performing system calls, and handling interrupts.

- Device Drivers: Writing device drivers is an important aspect of low-level programming. Device drivers enable communication between hardware devices and the operating system, allowing applications to utilize the functionalities provided by the devices.

- System-Level Optimization: Low-level programming is often employed to optimize performance-critical code. By understanding the low-level details of the hardware and

193

operating system, developers can fine-tune their code to take advantage of system-level optimizations and achieve better performance.

- Operating System Development: Building an operating system requires a deep understanding of low-level programming concepts. Operating systems are responsible for managing resources, scheduling tasks, providing services, and facilitating communication between various components of the system.

Benefits and Challenges of Low-Level Programming:

Low-level programming offers several benefits and challenges:

- Control and Efficiency: Low-level programming provides developers with fine-grained control over system resources, enabling them to optimize performance and implement custom functionalities.

- Understanding System Internals: Low-level programming enhances developers' understanding of how the hardware and operating system work together, leading to better insights into system behavior and performance bottlenecks.

- Complexity and Risk: Working at a low level introduces complexity and increases the risk of introducing bugs and vulnerabilities. Developers must be meticulous and aware of potential risks associated with direct system access.

- Portability: Low-level code is often platform-dependent and may require modifications when targeting different hardware or operating systems.

Real-World Applications of Low-Level Programming:

Low-level programming with C++ finds application in various domains, including:

- Embedded Systems: Embedded systems require low-level programming to interact with specialized hardware components and meet stringent resource constraints.

- Game Development: Game engines often employ low-level programming techniques for performance optimizations and platform-specific features.

- Real-Time Systems: Real-time systems, such as control systems and robotics, rely on low-level programming to ensure timely and deterministic response to external events.

- Security and Exploit Development: Understanding low-level programming is crucial for security researchers and exploit developers to identify vulnerabilities and develop countermeasures.

Low-level programming offers direct access to system resources, enabling control, efficiency, and system-level optimizations. It is essential for tasks such as device driver development, operating system development, and performance optimization. While low-level programming provides powerful capabilities, it also comes with complexity and requires meticulous attention to detail. By mastering low-level programming with C++, developers can unlock a realm of possibilities and gain a deeper understanding of how software interacts with hardware and operating systems.

Practical Examples of Low-Level Programming in C++

Low-level programming in C++ often involves direct interaction with the hardware or the operating system, manipulation of memory, or the use of specific programming techniques for optimization. Here are some practical examples of low-level programming tasks in C++.

Memory Management

C++ allows direct manipulation of memory through pointers. This is often used for dynamic memory allocation, where memory for variables is allocated at runtime. Here's an example of dynamic memory allocation for an array in C++:

```
int* arr = new int[10];  // Allocate memory for an array of 10 integers
for (int i = 0; i < 10; i++) {
    arr[i] = i;  // Assign values to the array
}
delete[] arr;  // Don't forget to free the memory when you're done!
```

Bit Manipulation

Bit manipulation is another area where C++ shines. This is often used in systems programming, cryptography, and graphics. Here's an example of using bitwise operators to manipulate bits in an integer:

```
unsigned int x = 15;  // Binary: 00001111
```

unsigned int y = x << 2; // Left shift by 2 bits: 00111100 (decimal 60)

Inline Assembly

C++ allows the use of inline assembly, where you can write assembly language code directly within your C++ code. This is often used for tasks that require direct control over the CPU, such as in systems programming or high-performance computing. Here's an example of using inline assembly to add two integers:

```
int add(int a, int b) {
    int result;
    __asm__ ("addl %%ebx, %%eax;"  // Assembly instruction
        : "=a" (result)  // Output operand
        : "a" (a), "b" (b)  // Input operands
        );
    return result;
}
```

Interfacing with Hardware

Low-level programming is often required when interfacing directly with hardware. This could involve writing device drivers, where you need to interact directly with the hardware of a specific device. While writing a device driver is beyond the scope of this example, it typically involves reading and writing to specific memory addresses, using system calls to interact with the operating system, and using interrupts to handle events from the device.

Optimizing Code

Low-level programming techniques can be used to optimize code for performance. This could involve techniques such as loop unrolling, using specific CPU instructions, or manipulating memory in a way that takes advantage of the cache architecture of the CPU.

Chapter 5: Complex C++ Constructs

Introduction to More Advanced Constructs in C++

C++ is a versatile language that offers a wide range of advanced constructs that allow for more efficient and flexible programming. These constructs include templates, the Standard Template Library (STL), exception handling, namespaces, and more. Let's delve into these advanced constructs.

Templates

Templates are a powerful feature of C++ that allows for generic programming. They enable you to write a single function or class that can work with different data types. For example, you can write a function template to implement a generic **max()** function that works with any type that can be compared:

```cpp
template <typename T>
T max(T a, T b) {
    return (a > b) ? a : b;
}
```

Standard Template Library (STL)

The Standard Template Library (STL) is a library in C++ that provides several generic classes and functions. This includes collections of algorithms, containers, iterators, and function objects. The STL can greatly reduce the amount of code you have to write and is often more efficient and reliable than custom code.

For example, the **std::vector** is a dynamic array provided by the STL:

```cpp
std::vector<int> vec;
vec.push_back(10);
```

vec.push_back(20);

Exception Handling

Exception handling in C++ provides a way to react to exceptional circumstances (like runtime errors) and continue running. This is done using the **try**, **catch**, **throw**, and **finally** keywords:

```
try {
    // Code that could throw an exception
    throw std::runtime_error("A problem occurred");
}
catch (const std::runtime_error& e) {
    // Handle the exception
    std::cerr << "Caught exception: " << e.what() << '\n';
}
```

Namespaces

Namespaces in C++ are used to group named entities (like classes, variables, and functions) that are logically related. They provide a way to avoid name collisions that can occur especially when your code base includes multiple libraries.

```
namespace MyNamespace {
    int x;
    int y;
}


int main() {
    MyNamespace::x = 10;
    MyNamespace::y = 20;
    return 0;
}
```

Object-Oriented Programming (OOP)

While not strictly an "advanced" construct, OOP in C++ is a vast topic that includes more advanced features like inheritance, polymorphism, abstract classes, and interfaces. These features allow for more modular and scalable code.

```cpp
class Base {
public:
  virtual void print() {
    std::cout << "Base" << std::endl;
  }
};


class Derived : public Base {
public:
  void print() override {
    std::cout << "Derived" << std::endl;
  }
};
```

C++ provides a wide range of advanced constructs that allow for powerful, flexible, and efficient programming. These constructs can make your code more modular, reusable, and maintainable, and they can help you tackle more complex programming tasks.

Understanding the Use of Classes, Objects, and Methods in C++

Classes, objects, and methods are fundamental concepts in object-oriented programming (OOP), and C++ is a language that fully supports OOP. Understanding these concepts is crucial for designing and implementing complex software systems.

Classes

A class in C++ is a user-defined data type that encapsulates data and functions that operate on that data. It serves as a blueprint for creating objects. A class is defined using the **class** keyword, followed by the name of the class and a block of code enclosed in curly braces {}.

Here's an example of a simple class definition:

class MyClass {

public:

  int myVariable; // A data member

  void myFunction() { // A member function (method)

    // Some code

  }

};

In this example, **MyClass** has one data member (**myVariable**) and one member function (**myFunction**).

Objects

An object is an instance of a class. When a class is defined, no memory is allocated. Memory is allocated only when objects are created. An object encapsulates the data and functions defined by the class.

You can create an object of a class like this:

MyClass myObject;

Now **myObject** is an object of **MyClass**, and you can access the data members and member functions of the class using the dot operator **.**:

myObject.myVariable = 10;

myObject.myFunction();

Methods

Methods, also known as member functions, are functions that belong to a class. They operate on the data members of the class. In the **MyClass** example above, **myFunction** is a method of **MyClass**.

Methods are defined in the body of the class and can be invoked on objects of the class. They can have access to the private data members of the class, which makes them a key part of encapsulation - one of the fundamental principles of OOP.

Here's how you might define and use a method that operates on a class's data:

```cpp
class MyClass {
public:
    int myVariable;

    void setVariable(int value) {
        myVariable = value;
    }

    int getVariable() {
        return myVariable;
    }
};


int main() {
    MyClass myObject;
    myObject.setVariable(10);
    std::cout << myObject.getVariable() << std::endl;  // Outputs: 10
    return 0;
}
```

In this example, **setVariable** and **getVariable** are methods that set and get the value of **myVariable**, respectively.

Chapter 6: Practical C++ Applications

Overview of Real-World Applications of C++

C++ is widely used in industries and domains that require high performance, efficiency, and low-level control. Its versatility and extensive library support make it an excellent choice for developing a wide range of applications. In this chapter, we explore some of the key areas where C++ finds practical use.

Systems Programming

C++ is extensively used in systems programming to develop operating systems, device drivers, embedded systems, and other software that interacts directly with hardware. Its ability to work at a low level and provide close control over memory and hardware resources makes it a preferred language for developing efficient and reliable system-level software.

Game Development

C++ is a popular choice for game development due to its ability to handle complex calculations, real-time graphics rendering, and resource management. Many game engines, such as Unreal Engine and Unity, are implemented in C++. Game developers leverage the performance and control offered by C++ to create immersive, high-performance games for various platforms.

High-Performance Computing

C++ is widely used in high-performance computing (HPC) applications, such as scientific simulations, computational fluid dynamics, financial modeling, and data analysis. Its ability to efficiently handle large datasets and perform complex computations makes it ideal for applications that require substantial computational power.

Networking and Telecommunications

C++ is often used in networking and telecommunications applications that demand low-latency and high-throughput processing. It enables the development of network protocols, server applications, routers, and other networking components. C++ libraries like Boost.Asio provide a robust framework for building network applications.

Financial Systems

The financial industry heavily relies on C++ for developing algorithmic trading systems, risk management tools, high-frequency trading platforms, and other financial applications. C++'s performance, control over memory, and support for mathematical libraries make it well-suited for processing large volumes of financial data and executing complex calculations.

Scientific and Engineering Software

C++ is widely used in scientific and engineering domains for developing simulation software, data analysis tools, and modeling applications. Its ability to work with complex mathematical algorithms, numerical libraries, and performance optimization techniques makes it an ideal choice for these applications.

Graphical User Interface (GUI) Development

C++ offers several libraries and frameworks for building graphical user interfaces. Popular libraries like Qt and wxWidgets enable the creation of cross-platform desktop applications with rich and interactive user interfaces. C++'s efficiency and flexibility make it suitable for developing GUI applications with demanding graphical requirements.

From systems programming to game development, high-performance computing to financial systems, and scientific software to GUI development, C++ proves to be a versatile language capable of addressing diverse real-world challenges.

Hands-on Projects to Understand C++'s Practical Application

These projects provide a practical understanding of how C++ can be used in real-world scenarios and reinforce your learning by engaging in hands-on coding exercises. By working on these projects, you will gain valuable experience and confidence in using C++ to build practical applications.

Console-Based Calculator

Develop a console-based calculator application that performs basic arithmetic operations such as addition, subtraction, multiplication, and division. This project will give you a solid understanding of C++ syntax, data types, and control structures. You'll learn how to handle user input, perform calculations, and display results on the console.

File Management System

Create a file management system that allows users to perform basic file operations such as creating, reading, updating, and deleting files. This project will involve working with file input/output (I/O) operations, manipulating file data, and implementing error handling techniques. You'll gain insights into file handling concepts and learn how to manage files efficiently using C++.

Student Record Management

Build a student record management system that allows users to store and retrieve student information such as name, age, and grades. This project will involve designing classes, implementing object-oriented programming principles, and utilizing data structures like arrays or linked lists to store and manipulate student data. You'll gain practical experience in using classes and objects to model real-world entities.

Simple Game

Develop a simple game, such as a guessing game or a tic-tac-toe game, using C++. This project will introduce you to game development concepts, including user input handling, game logic, and control flow. You'll learn how to structure and organize code for a game, implement game rules, and provide an interactive gaming experience.

Image Processing Application

Create an image processing application that allows users to apply various image filters, such as grayscale conversion, brightness adjustment, and edge detection. This project will involve working with image file formats, understanding pixel manipulation, and implementing image processing algorithms. You'll explore the intersection of C++ and computer graphics, gaining insights into image processing techniques.

Bank Management System

Design a bank management system that simulates banking operations such as account creation, deposits, withdrawals, and balance inquiries. This project will focus on designing classes, managing data structures for customer accounts, and implementing transactional operations. You'll gain experience in modeling real-world systems and understanding the importance of data integrity and security.

By engaging in these projects, you will enhance your problem-solving skills, gain confidence in using C++ to build real-world applications, and reinforce your understanding of key concepts. These projects will help you develop a portfolio of practical C++ applications, demonstrating your proficiency to potential employers or showcasing your abilities to peers in the programming community. Embrace the opportunity to explore C++'s practical applications and unleash your creativity in solving real-world challenges.

Chapter 7: Next Steps in C++

Preparing for Advanced Topics in C++

This chapter serves as a guide to help you prepare for advanced topics in C++ and lays the foundation for further exploration into the language. By familiarizing yourself with these concepts, you'll be ready to tackle more complex projects and delve into advanced C++ programming techniques.

Object-Oriented Programming (OOP) Principles

To advance in C++, it's crucial to have a solid understanding of object-oriented programming principles. Review and deepen your knowledge of concepts such as encapsulation, inheritance, and polymorphism. OOP provides a powerful paradigm for designing modular, reusable, and maintainable code. By mastering these principles, you'll be well-equipped to create sophisticated and scalable applications.

Templates and Generic Programming

Templates and generic programming enable you to write reusable code that can adapt to different data types. Dive into the world of template programming, where you'll learn about function templates, class templates, and template specialization. Explore the advantages of generic programming in terms of code reusability and type safety. This knowledge will open doors to building versatile libraries and frameworks.

Standard Template Library (STL)

The Standard Template Library is a collection of powerful containers, algorithms, and iterators provided by the C++ Standard Library. Understand the various containers, such as vectors, lists, and maps, and how to use them effectively in your programs. Learn about the STL algorithms, which allow you to perform operations like sorting, searching, and manipulating data effortlessly. The STL is an indispensable tool for C++ developers, and mastering it will greatly enhance your programming capabilities.

Memory Management

Memory management is a critical aspect of C++ programming, especially when dealing with dynamic memory allocation. Explore topics such as pointers, memory allocation operators (new and delete), and memory leaks. Understand the differences between stack and heap memory and learn best practices for efficient memory management. This knowledge will help you write robust and memory-efficient code.

Exception Handling

Exception handling is a vital technique for handling errors and exceptional situations in your programs. Learn how to use try-catch blocks to handle exceptions and gracefully recover from errors. Gain insights into exception hierarchy, custom exception classes, and exception safety guarantees. Effective exception handling ensures the reliability and stability of your applications.

Advanced C++ Features

Prepare to explore advanced features of C++ such as lambda expressions, move semantics, smart pointers, and multithreading. Lambda expressions provide concise and powerful ways to define inline functions. Move semantics and smart pointers enable efficient resource management. Multithreading allows you to leverage the full potential of modern hardware by parallelizing your code. Familiarize yourself with these features to take your C++ programming to the next level.

By preparing yourself with a solid understanding of object-oriented programming principles, templates, the Standard Template Library, memory management, exception handling, and advanced C++ features, you'll be ready to tackle more complex projects and explore specialized areas of C++ programming. Embrace the opportunity to deepen your understanding of the language and continue expanding your skills. With this knowledge, you'll be well-equipped to tackle advanced C++ concepts and build robust, efficient, and scalable applications.

Suggestions for Continued Learning and Practice

These suggestions will help you explore additional resources, gain real-world experience, and continue to improve your C++ programming abilities.

Read C++ Books and Online Resources

Continue expanding your knowledge of C++ by reading books and exploring online resources. Look for advanced C++ books that cover topics like design patterns, algorithms, and optimization techniques. These resources can provide in-depth explanations, examples, and insights from experienced C++ developers. Additionally, explore online forums, blogs, and tutorials that focus on advanced C++ concepts and problem-solving techniques. Regularly engaging with new content will keep you updated on the latest developments in the C++ community.

Contribute to Open-Source Projects

Participating in open-source projects is an excellent way to gain real-world experience and collaborate with other developers. Look for C++ projects on platforms like GitHub and contribute to their development. By working with experienced developers and contributing code to open-source projects, you'll gain valuable insights into industry best practices, code review processes, and collaborative development workflows. It's also an opportunity to showcase your skills and build a strong portfolio.

Solve Challenging Programming Problems

Challenge yourself by solving complex programming problems in C++. Platforms like LeetCode, HackerRank, and Project Euler offer a wide range of programming challenges that will test your problem-solving skills and deepen your understanding of advanced C++ concepts. These platforms often provide detailed explanations and discussions for each problem, allowing you to learn from others and expand your problem-solving techniques.

Collaborate on C++ Projects

Collaborate with fellow C++ enthusiasts or join programming communities to work on C++ projects together. By collaborating with others, you'll gain exposure to different coding styles, learn new techniques, and receive feedback on your code. Consider participating in coding competitions or hackathons where you can work on time-constrained projects with a team. Collaborative projects provide valuable opportunities for learning, networking, and building teamwork skills.

Explore Advanced Topics and Specializations

C++ is a versatile language with various advanced topics and specializations. Consider exploring areas such as game development with C++ and game engines like Unreal Engine or Unity, scientific computing with libraries like Boost and Eigen, or embedded systems programming. Choose a specialization that aligns with your interests and career goals, and delve deeper into that particular domain. This focused exploration will enhance your expertise and make you stand out as a C++ professional.

Build and Refine Personal Projects

Continue building personal projects to apply and reinforce your C++ knowledge. Identify areas where you can improve and expand your projects. Consider refactoring and optimizing existing code, implementing new features, or integrating third-party libraries. Building and refining personal projects will help you gain practical experience and solidify your understanding of C++ programming principles and best practices.

By engaging in ongoing learning, contributing to open-source projects, solving challenging programming problems, collaborating on C++ projects, exploring advanced topics and specializations, and building and refining personal projects, you'll continue to enhance your C++ skills and become a proficient programmer. Remember to stay curious, be persistent in your learning, and embrace new challenges. With dedication and practice, you'll continue to grow as a C++ developer and unlock exciting opportunities in the field of programming.

Book 5 - C++ Programming: Mastering Complex Structures and Database Management

Introduction: Advancing in C++

Preparing for Advanced Topics in C++

As you progress in your journey to master complex structures and database management in C++, it is important to lay a strong foundation and acquire the necessary knowledge to tackle more sophisticated concepts.

Before diving into advanced topics, it is crucial to ensure a solid understanding of the fundamentals of C++. Review the core concepts, such as variables, data types, control structures, functions, and object-oriented programming principles. Reinforce your knowledge by practicing basic programming exercises and familiarizing yourself with the common syntax and idioms of C++. A strong grasp of the fundamentals will serve as a solid base for tackling more complex concepts.

To delve deeper into advanced topics, consider reading books specifically dedicated to advanced C++ programming. These books often cover topics such as template metaprogramming, multithreading, advanced data structures, and design patterns. Some recommended titles include "Effective Modern C++" by Scott Meyers, "C++ Concurrency in Action" by Anthony Williams, and "C++ Templates: The Complete Guide" by David Vandevoorde and Nicolai M. Josuttis. Additionally, explore online resources, tutorials, and articles that focus on advanced C++ topics. Keep up-to-date with the latest developments in the C++ community to stay ahead.

As you progress to more complex applications, understanding advanced data structures and algorithms becomes essential. Explore topics like linked lists, trees, graphs, sorting algorithms, searching algorithms, and dynamic programming. Implement these data structures and algorithms in C++ to reinforce your understanding and improve your problem-solving skills. Practice solving challenging programming problems that require the application of these advanced concepts. Platforms like LeetCode, Codeforces, and HackerRank offer a vast collection of algorithmic challenges to help you sharpen your skills.

To master complex structures and database management, familiarize yourself with database concepts and DBMS tools. Learn about relational databases, SQL (Structured Query Language), and database design principles. Understand how to interact with databases using C++ by leveraging libraries like SQLite or connecting to external database servers through APIs. Explore topics such as data modeling, query optimization, transaction management, and database security. Practical hands-on experience with database projects will deepen your understanding of how C++ integrates with DBMS.

To gain practical experience and solidify your understanding of advanced topics in C++, undertake real-world projects. Identify areas where you can apply your knowledge and challenge yourself. Consider developing applications that involve complex data structures, algorithmic problem-solving, and database interactions. Collaborate with others or contribute to open-source projects related to your areas of interest. By working on practical projects, you will encounter real-world challenges, refine your skills, and learn from practical scenarios.

Engage with the C++ community to foster continuous learning and growth. Participate in forums, discussion boards, and online communities where C++ developers share their knowledge and experiences. Attend C++ conferences, workshops, and meetups to network with professionals and learn from industry experts. Engaging with the community will expose you to different perspectives, new techniques, and emerging trends in the C++ ecosystem.

Preparing for advanced topics in C++ is an exciting phase in your journey to becoming a proficient C++ developer. By strengthening your fundamentals, exploring advanced books and resources, studying advanced data structures and algorithms, understanding database management systems, engaging in real-world projects, and staying active in the C++ community, you will equip yourself with the necessary skills and knowledge to tackle complex structures and database management with confidence. Remember, continuous learning and practical application are key to mastering advanced topics in C++. Embrace the challenges, remain persistent, and enjoy the journey of advancing in C++.

The Evolving Position of C++ in the Programming Market and Its Current Use Cases

As you embark on the journey of mastering complex structures and database management in C++, it is essential to understand the evolving position of this programming language in the market and its current use cases. C++ has a rich history and has continually evolved to meet the demands of modern software development.

Widely Used in System Programming

C++ has long been recognized as a language of choice for system programming. Its low-level capabilities, efficiency, and ability to interact with hardware make it well-suited for developing operating systems, device drivers, embedded systems, and real-time applications. C++ allows developers to have fine-grained control over memory management and provides direct access to hardware resources, making it indispensable in domains where performance and control are critical.

High-Performance Computing and Scientific Applications

C++ is extensively used in high-performance computing (HPC) and scientific computing applications. Its ability to optimize code execution, leverage multithreading, and utilize low-level programming constructs make it suitable for computationally intensive tasks. C++ is often used in areas such as numerical simulations, weather forecasting, molecular modeling, and computational finance, where the efficient utilization of computing resources is paramount.

Game Development

The gaming industry heavily relies on C++ for developing cutting-edge games. C++ offers the performance required for rendering complex graphics, implementing physics engines, and managing game logic. Game engines like Unreal Engine and Unity are built using C++ and provide developers with powerful frameworks for creating immersive gaming experiences. C++'s support for object-oriented programming and its ability to interface with other languages make it a preferred choice for game development.

Database Management Systems

C++ plays a crucial role in database management systems (DBMS) and data-intensive applications. C++ is used to build efficient and scalable database engines, query optimizers, and data processing frameworks. Its ability to manipulate memory efficiently and work with complex data structures makes it well-suited for managing large volumes of data. C++ libraries like MySQL and PostgreSQL provide robust and performant solutions for handling database operations.

Financial and Trading Systems

The financial industry heavily relies on C++ for developing trading systems, algorithmic trading platforms, and high-frequency trading applications. C++'s ability to handle complex calculations, process large amounts of financial data, and maintain low latency is crucial in this domain. C++'s performance, combined with its support for multi-threading and real-time data processing, makes it a natural choice for building reliable and efficient financial systems.

Infrastructure Software

C++ is widely used in the development of infrastructure software, including networking protocols, communication libraries, compilers, and operating system components. Its ability to work at a low level and interface with different hardware and software components enables the creation of robust and efficient infrastructure solutions. C++'s support for concurrent programming and its low-level control make it indispensable in the development of critical system-level software.

C++ continues to play a vital role in the programming market and offers a diverse range of use cases. Its position as a language for system programming, high-performance computing, game development, database management systems, financial applications, and infrastructure software highlights its versatility and power. As you advance in C++ and explore complex structures and database management, understanding the current use cases and market demands will help you leverage the language effectively. Embrace the opportunities that C++ provides in these domains and continue honing your skills to become a proficient C++ developer in your chosen field.

Chapter 1: The Role of C++ in High-Performance and Core Projects

Exploring the Strength of C++ in Developing High-Performance, Machine-Based Solutions

We delve into the role of C++ in high-performance and core projects, focusing on its strength in developing high-performance, machine-based solutions. C++ is a powerful programming language known for its efficiency, performance, and low-level capabilities. Its ability to work with complex structures and manage databases makes it a preferred choice for building robust and scalable applications. Let's explore how C++ excels in developing high-performance solutions for machine-based applications.

Performance and Efficiency

C++ is renowned for its performance and efficiency. It offers direct memory management and control, enabling developers to optimize their code and achieve high execution speeds. C++ code can be finely tuned and tailored to specific hardware architectures, taking advantage of low-level optimizations such as manual memory management and inline assembly. This level of control and optimization is crucial in high-performance computing, where every bit of speed counts.

Low-Level Access

One of the primary strengths of C++ is its ability to provide low-level access to the hardware. This is particularly useful in machine-based solutions, where direct interaction with hardware devices or machine components is necessary. C++ allows developers to write code that interacts directly with the underlying system, making it ideal for developing drivers, firmware, and other systems-level software.

Integration with Existing Codebases

C++ is often used to integrate existing codebases, especially those written in lower-level languages like C or assembly. Its compatibility with C code enables seamless integration with libraries and frameworks written in C, expanding the capabilities and functionality of existing projects. This flexibility makes C++ an excellent choice for extending or optimizing legacy systems and integrating them with modern machine-based solutions.

Parallelism and Multithreading

C++ provides robust support for parallelism and multithreading, making it suitable for high-performance applications that require efficient utilization of multiple cores or processors. C++ offers standard libraries like the Thread Support Library and the Parallel Algorithms Library, which enable developers to write concurrent and parallel code. This capability is crucial in machine-based solutions that involve processing vast amounts of data or running complex computations.

Handling Complex Data Structures

Machine-based solutions often deal with large and complex data structures, such as databases or intricate data models. C++ provides the necessary tools and constructs to handle these structures efficiently. It offers features like templates, classes, and strong type safety, enabling developers to build robust data structures and manipulate them with ease. This capability is particularly valuable in database management systems, where efficiency and reliability are paramount.

Scalability and Extensibility

C++ is known for its scalability and extensibility, making it suitable for developing large-scale, enterprise-level applications. Its modular nature and support for object-oriented programming allow for the creation of reusable and maintainable codebases. C++'s ability to build complex structures and its support for libraries and frameworks make it an excellent choice for developing extensible and scalable solutions.

C++'s strength in developing high-performance, machine-based solutions lies in its performance, low-level access, integration capabilities, parallelism support, handling of complex data structures, and scalability. As you embark on mastering complex structures and database management in C++, understanding the language's capabilities and strengths in high-performance computing is crucial. By leveraging C++'s efficiency, low-level control, and compatibility with existing codebases, you can develop powerful and performant solutions for machine-based applications. Keep exploring the possibilities and continue honing your skills to become a proficient developer in C++ for high-performance and core projects.

Reviewing Real-World Examples of C++ in Core Project Development

C++ is widely used in various industries to build critical systems and applications that require efficiency, performance, and reliability. By examining these examples, we gain insights into how C++ is leveraged to tackle complex challenges and achieve optimal results in core project development.

Operating Systems

One notable real-world example of C++ in core project development is the development of operating systems. C++ is often used to build the kernel, device drivers, and other critical components of an operating system. Its low-level capabilities, such as direct memory management and hardware access, make it well-suited for developing efficient and robust operating systems.

Game Engines

Game development is another domain where C++ plays a significant role. Game engines, which are the foundation of modern game development, heavily rely on C++ to achieve high performance and real-time rendering. C++ allows developers to optimize code for specific hardware platforms, utilize multithreading for parallel processing, and handle complex graphics and physics calculations. Many popular game engines, such as Unreal Engine and Unity, are predominantly written in C++.

Embedded Systems

C++ is widely used in the development of embedded systems, which are computer systems embedded within other devices or machines. These systems range from small microcontrollers to complex systems in automotive, aerospace, and industrial applications. C++ enables efficient control of hardware resources, implementation of real-time functionality, and management of memory constraints. It is used to build firmware, control systems, and communication protocols for a wide range of embedded devices.

Financial Systems

The financial industry relies on high-performance systems for trading, risk management, and algorithmic trading. C++ is a popular choice for building these systems due to its efficiency, low latency, and ability to handle large volumes of data. C++ allows developers to create complex data structures, implement mathematical models, and interact with financial data sources. The performance and reliability of C++ make it a preferred language for developing robust financial systems.

Networking and Telecommunications

C++ is widely used in the development of networking and telecommunications applications. Networking protocols, routers, switches, and communication frameworks are often implemented using C++. C++ enables developers to handle low-level network programming, manage network resources, and ensure optimal performance. Its ability to work with sockets, manage data packets, and handle concurrent connections makes it well-suited for networking applications.

Database Management Systems

C++ is utilized in the development of database management systems (DBMS) that handle large-scale data storage and retrieval. C++ provides the necessary tools to build efficient data structures, handle complex queries, and manage memory effectively. DBMS written in C++ offer high performance, concurrency control, and scalability required for handling vast amounts of structured and unstructured data.

Real-world examples of C++ in core project development demonstrate its versatility, performance, and suitability for building critical systems and applications. Whether it's operating systems, game engines, embedded systems, financial systems, networking and telecommunications applications, or database management systems, C++ excels in delivering high-performance solutions. By studying and understanding these examples, you gain insights into the power and potential of C++ in mastering complex structures and database management. As you progress in your C++ journey, exploring and applying the principles and techniques from these real-world examples will enhance your skills and enable you to tackle complex projects with confidence.

Chapter 2: Advanced C++ Features: Templates, STL, and Boost Libraries

Deep Dive into Advanced Features of C++, including Templates and the Standard Template Library (STL)

Two key components we will delve into are templates and the Standard Template Library (STL). These features enhance the capabilities of C++ by enabling code reusability, generic programming, and efficient data structures and algorithms. Understanding and harnessing these advanced features is crucial for mastering complex structures and database management in C++.

Templates

Templates are a powerful feature in C++ that facilitate generic programming. They enable the creation of reusable code that can work with different data types. By writing generic algorithms and data structures, developers can achieve greater code flexibility and reduce code duplication. Templates allow the creation of functions and classes that operate on multiple types, providing a high level of abstraction and code reusability.

Within the realm of complex structures and database management, templates can be utilized to implement generic data structures such as linked lists, binary trees, hash tables, and queues. These data structures can then be used to efficiently organize and manipulate complex data in a database system. Templates also play a significant role in database management systems by enabling the creation of generic algorithms for data querying, sorting, and manipulation.

Standard Template Library (STL)

The Standard Template Library (STL) is a collection of template classes and functions that form a part of the C++ Standard Library. It provides a comprehensive set of reusable algorithms, containers, and iterators, which greatly simplify the implementation of complex data structures and algorithms.

The STL includes various container classes such as vectors, lists, queues, and maps, which offer efficient storage and retrieval of data. Algorithms like sorting, searching, and manipulating data are also provided by the STL, allowing developers to perform complex operations with ease. Additionally, the STL provides powerful iterators that enable efficient traversal and manipulation of container elements.

The integration of STL in complex structure and database management projects can significantly enhance their efficiency and maintainability. By leveraging the STL, developers can utilize proven algorithms and data structures, reducing the need for custom implementations and improving code quality and performance.

Boost Libraries

Apart from templates and the STL, another valuable resource for advanced C++ development is the Boost Libraries. Boost is a widely used collection of high-quality, peer-reviewed libraries that extend the capabilities of C++. These libraries cover various domains such as math, filesystem, networking, and multithreading, providing developers with additional tools and functionalities.

The Boost Libraries offer an extensive set of tools that can be beneficial for mastering complex structures and database management. For example, the Boost Graph Library provides data structures and algorithms for graph-based structures, which are fundamental in database modeling and management. Boost.Asio enables efficient networking capabilities, which can be crucial for building distributed database systems. These libraries, along with many others in the Boost collection, expand the possibilities and performance of C++ in complex projects.

These features empower developers to write efficient, reusable, and flexible code for mastering complex structures and database management. Templates enable generic programming, reducing code duplication and increasing code reusability. The STL provides a rich collection of containers, algorithms, and iterators, simplifying the implementation of complex data structures and algorithms. The Boost Libraries further extend the capabilities of C++ with additional functionalities and tools.

By understanding and applying these advanced features, developers can unlock the full potential of C++ in complex projects. Templates, the STL, and the Boost Libraries provide the necessary tools and abstractions to tackle complex structures, algorithms, and database management tasks efficiently. Embracing these features expands the possibilities of C++ development, facilitating the creation of high-performance and robust solutions.

Understanding and Using the Boost Libraries in C++

Boost is a collection of around 80 libraries that extend the functionality of C++. These libraries are open-source and are available for everyone to use and contribute to. They are designed to work well with the C++ Standard Library and provide facilities that are not available in the standard library. Many of the libraries in Boost have been incorporated into the C++ Standard Library over the years, such as smart pointers, regular expressions, and threading.

The Boost libraries cover a wide range of programming needs, including string and text processing, containers, iterators, algorithms, input/output, and more. They are designed to be portable across many different platforms and operating systems, and to work well with a wide variety of compilers.

Setting Up Boost

Before you can use Boost, you need to download and install it. The Boost website (www.boost.org) provides detailed instructions for various platforms. Once Boost is installed, you can include the necessary libraries in your C++ program with the **#include** directive. For example, to use the Boost.Regex library, you would include it like this:

#include <boost/regex.hpp>

Using Boost Libraries

Here are some examples of how to use some of the most popular Boost libraries:

Boost.Asio for Network and Low-Level I/O Programming

Boost.Asio is a cross-platform C++ library for network and low-level I/O programming. It provides a consistent asynchronous model using a modern C++ approach. This makes it easier to write networked applications, as it handles many of the low-level details for you.

Here's a simple example of creating a timer with Boost.Asio:

```
#include <boost/asio.hpp>
#include <iostream>


int main() {
    boost::asio::io_context io;
    boost::asio::steady_timer t(io, boost::asio::chrono::seconds(5));
    t.wait();
    std::cout << "Hello, world!" << std::endl;
    return 0;
}
```

In this example, we first create an **io_context** object. This object is used by Boost.Asio to interact with the operating system's I/O services. We then create a **steady_timer** object, which represents a timer. We set the timer to expire in 5 seconds. The **wait()** function blocks until the timer has expired. After the timer has expired, we print "Hello, world!" to the console.

Boost.Filesystem for Filesystem Operations

Boost.Filesystem provides a portable way to interact with the filesystem. It can be used to create, delete, or inspect files and directories. It also provides functions for path manipulation and file I/O.

Here's a simple example of using Boost.Filesystem to get the size of a file:

```
#include <boost/filesystem.hpp>
#include <iostream>


int main() {
```

```
boost::filesystem::path p("my_file.txt");
if (boost::filesystem::exists(p)) {
    std::cout << boost::filesystem::file_size(p) << std::endl;
}
return 0;
}
```

In this example, we first create a **path** object, which represents a path in the filesystem. We then check if the path exists with the **exists**() function. If the path exists, we print its size to the console with the **file_size**() function.

Boost.Regex for Regular Expressions

Boost.Regex provides regular expression support. Regular expressions are a powerful tool for processing text. They allow you to match and manipulate strings based on patterns.

Here's a simple example of using Boost.Regex to match a string:

```
#include <boost/regex.hpp>
#include <iostream>

int main() {
    std::string line;
    boost::regex pat("^Subject: (Re: |Aw: )*(.*)");

    while (std::cin) {
        std::getline(std::cin, line);
        boost::smatch matches;
        if (boost::regex_match(line, matches, pat))
            std::cout << matches[2] << std::endl;
    }
    return 0;
}
```

In this example, we first create a **regex** object, which represents a regular expression. We then read lines from the standard input with **std::getline**(). For each line, we try to match it against the regular expression with the **regex_match**() function. If the line matches the regular expression, we print the second match to the console.

Chapter 3: C++ Optimization Techniques

Techniques for Optimizing C++ Code for Better Performance

Optimizing C++ code for better performance involves a combination of good coding practices, efficient algorithms and data structures, and understanding the hardware and compiler. Here are some techniques for optimizing C++ code.

Choose the Right Algorithm and Data Structure

The choice of algorithm and data structure is fundamental to the performance of your code. Different algorithms and data structures have different time and space complexities, which describe how their resource usage scales with the size of the input.

For example, if you're performing a lot of searches in a collection of items, a linear search in an array has a time complexity of O(n), meaning the time it takes increases linearly with the number of items. However, if those items are in a sorted array or a balanced binary search tree, you can use a binary search with a time complexity of O(log n), which is much faster for large collections. Similarly, different data structures are optimal for different kinds of tasks. If you frequently need to look up values by a key, a hash table (such as **std::unordered_map**) can perform lookups in constant time on average, while a binary search tree (such as **std::map**) performs lookups in logarithmic time.

Avoid Unnecessary Copying

Copying can be a costly operation, especially for large objects. Every time an object is copied, all of its data must be duplicated, which takes time and memory. If you're passing objects to a function, consider passing by reference or by pointer instead of by value to avoid copying. If a function needs to return an object, consider returning by value and relying on Return Value

Optimization (RVO) or Named Return Value Optimization (NRVO), compiler optimizations that eliminate the overhead of returning an object by value.

In C++11 and later, you can also use move semantics to "move" resources from one object to another, without having to copy and delete them. This can significantly improve performance for types that manage expensive resources, like **std::vector** or **std::string**.

Use Inline Functions

Function calls have a certain overhead. The function's arguments must be pushed onto the stack, control must be transferred to the function, and then when the function is done, control must be transferred back and the stack must be cleaned up. Inlining a function can eliminate this overhead by replacing the function call with the function's code.

However, inlining a function increases the size of the binary, as the function's code is duplicated each time the function is called. This can lead to code bloat and can potentially hurt performance by causing more cache misses. Therefore, it's generally best to only inline small functions that are called frequently.

Use const and constexpr Where Appropriate

The **const** keyword tells the compiler that a variable's value will not change after it is initialized. This allows the compiler to make certain optimizations, like replacing uses of the variable with its value.

The **constexpr** keyword tells the compiler to evaluate an expression at compile time. This can be used to compute values that are known at compile time, saving time at runtime.

Optimize Loop Performance

Loops are a common source of performance bottlenecks, as they can cause a section of code to be executed many times. There are several techniques for optimizing loops:

- **Loop Unrolling**: This technique involves increasing the number of operations in the loop body and decreasing the number of loop iterations. This reduces the overhead of loop control but increases the size of the code, which can lead to more instruction cache misses.

- **Loop Jamming**: This technique involves combining two or more loops that iterate over the same range into one loop. This reduces the overhead of loop control but can make the loop body more complex.

- **Loop Invariant Code Motion**: If a loop contains code that computes the same result in each iteration, that code can be moved outside the loop. This reduces the amount of work done in each iteration.

Use Compiler Optimizations

Modern compilers are capable of performing a wide range of optimizations. These include function inlining, loop unrolling, constant propagation, dead code elimination, and many more. By understanding these optimizations and writing code that can take advantage of them, you can improve the performance of your code without having to make significant changes.

Understand Cache Utilization

Modern CPUs have a hierarchy of caches (L1, L2, etc.). These caches store frequently accessed data and can be accessed much faster than main memory. By understanding how your code interacts with the cache, you can write code that maximizes cache hits and minimizes cache misses. This often involves organizing your data and computations to take advantage of spatial and temporal locality.

Use Multithreading and Concurrency

If your program performs tasks that can be done in parallel, using multithreading can significantly improve performance. This is especially true on modern multi-core processors, where each thread can run on a separate core. However, multithreaded programming can be complex and error-prone, and requires careful synchronization to avoid race conditions.

Profile Your Code

Profiling involves measuring the performance of your code to identify bottlenecks. This is typically done with a profiling tool, which measures things like CPU usage, memory usage, and I/O operations. By profiling your code, you can focus your optimization efforts on the parts of your code that have the most impact on performance.

Optimizing C++ code is crucial for achieving high performance in complex structure and database management scenarios. By applying profiling, benchmarking, algorithmic improvements, memory management techniques, compiler optimizations, and leveraging multithreading and parallelism, developers can unlock the full potential of their C++ applications. Utilizing the C++ Standard Library and third-party libraries can further enhance code efficiency. It is essential to balance optimization efforts with code readability, maintainability, and portability to ensure long-term success.

Understanding and Avoiding Common Performance Pitfalls in C++

C++ is a powerful language that provides a lot of control over system resources, but with that power comes responsibility. It's easy to inadvertently write code that performs poorly if you're not careful. Here are some common performance pitfalls in C++ and how to avoid them:

Unnecessary Copying

In C++, passing large objects by value can result in unnecessary copying, which can be costly in terms of performance. To avoid this, consider passing objects by reference or pointer instead. This is especially important for function parameters and return values.

For example, instead of:

void process(std::vector<int> v) { /*...*/ }

Consider:

void process(const std::vector<int>& v) { /*...*/ }

In C++11 and later, you can also use move semantics to avoid copying when you want to transfer ownership of resources.

Inefficient Use of Containers

Different containers have different performance characteristics. For example, inserting or removing elements in the middle of a **std::vector** is slow because all the elements after the insertion or removal point must be shifted. If you frequently insert or remove elements in the middle, consider using a **std::list** or **std::deque** instead.

Also, keep in mind that different containers have different memory usage characteristics. For example, a **std::list** uses more memory than a **std::vector** because it needs to store pointers to the next and previous elements.

Ignoring Cache Effects

Modern CPUs have a cache hierarchy to speed up memory access. If your data is small enough to fit in the cache and is accessed in a predictable pattern, your program can run significantly faster. However, if your data is too large or your access pattern is unpredictable, you may suffer from cache misses, which can slow down your program.

To write cache-friendly code, try to keep your data structures small and simple, and access memory in a sequential or otherwise predictable pattern.

Not Taking Advantage of Compiler Optimizations

Modern C++ compilers are capable of performing a wide range of optimizations that can significantly improve the performance of your code. However, these optimizations are often disabled in debug builds to make debugging easier.

To ensure your code runs as fast as possible, make sure to enable optimizations in your release builds. In GCC and Clang, you can do this with the **-O2** or **-O3** command-line options.

Blocking on I/O Operations

I/O operations, such as reading from a file or a network socket, are much slower than CPU operations. If your program blocks waiting for an I/O operation to complete, it can't do anything else in the meantime.

To avoid this, consider using asynchronous I/O operations, which allow your program to continue doing other work while the I/O operation is in progress. In C++11 and later, you can use the **std::async** function to easily perform operations asynchronously.

Unnecessary Heap Allocations

Allocating memory on the heap is much slower than allocating memory on the stack. If you frequently allocate and deallocate small objects on the heap, consider using a memory pool or a custom allocator to speed up these operations.

Also, keep in mind that each heap allocation has a memory overhead. If you have many small objects, this overhead can add up and consume a significant amount of memory.

While C++ gives you a lot of control over how your program uses system resources, it also requires you to be mindful of how you use those resources. By understanding and avoiding these common performance pitfalls, you can write C++ code that runs faster and uses less memory.

Chapter 4: Graphical Libraries and Visual Design in C++

Exploring the Use of Graphical Libraries in C++ and Their Applications in Visual Design

Graphical libraries provide a set of tools and functions that enable developers to create visually appealing and interactive user interfaces, graphics, and animations. By leveraging these libraries, developers can enhance the user experience and create visually compelling applications in various domains such as gaming, multimedia, data visualization, and more.

Overview of Graphical Libraries

C++ offers several powerful graphical libraries, each with its own set of features, capabilities, and focus areas. Some popular graphical libraries in C++ include Qt, OpenGL, SFML (Simple and Fast Multimedia Library), and SDL (Simple DirectMedia Layer). These libraries provide a wide range of functionality, including window management, rendering, event handling, multimedia support, and more. Understanding the capabilities and strengths of these libraries can help developers choose the most suitable one for their specific project requirements.

User Interface Design

Graphical libraries enable developers to create visually appealing user interfaces (UIs) for applications. They provide a wide range of UI elements such as buttons, menus, text fields, sliders, and checkboxes that can be customized and arranged to create intuitive and interactive interfaces. These libraries often include layout managers, style sheets, and theming options to facilitate the design process. Developers can leverage graphical libraries to create user-friendly interfaces that enhance the usability and aesthetics of their applications.

Graphics and Animation

Visual design goes beyond user interfaces. Graphical libraries in C++ allow developers to create and manipulate 2D and 3D graphics, apply transformations, render images, and work with shaders. They provide functionality for drawing shapes, lines, curves, and textures, as well as supporting advanced rendering techniques such as lighting and shading. Additionally, these libraries offer animation capabilities to bring graphics to life through smooth transitions, keyframe animations, and particle effects.

Multimedia Support

Many graphical libraries in C++ offer multimedia support, allowing developers to incorporate audio and video elements into their applications. They provide APIs for playing audio files, handling real-time audio input/output, and synchronizing multimedia content. This enables the creation of multimedia-rich applications, such as multimedia players, interactive presentations, and video games.

Data Visualization

Data visualization is a crucial aspect of many applications, especially in domains such as scientific research, data analysis, and business intelligence. Graphical libraries provide tools for visualizing data through charts, graphs, heatmaps, and other visual representations. Developers can leverage these libraries to create visually compelling and informative data visualizations that help users understand complex information and make informed decisions.

Cross-Platform Development

One of the advantages of using graphical libraries in C++ is their cross-platform compatibility. Many libraries support multiple operating systems, including Windows, macOS, Linux, and even mobile platforms like Android and iOS. This allows developers to write code once and deploy their applications on different platforms without significant modifications. Cross-platform development using graphical libraries can save development time and effort while reaching a wider audience.

These libraries provide a wealth of tools and functionality to create visually appealing user interfaces, graphics, animations, multimedia applications, and data visualizations. By leveraging graphical libraries, developers can enhance the user experience, create engaging applications, and effectively communicate complex information. Understanding the capabilities and features of graphical libraries empowers developers to unleash their creativity and create visually stunning applications using C++.

Practical Examples of ActiveX Controls and Game Development

ActiveX controls, game development, and other use cases represent a wide range of applications for programming and software development. Let's delve into each of these topics in more detail.

ActiveX Controls

ActiveX is a framework introduced by Microsoft in 1996 as a part of the Component Object Model (COM) and Object Linking and Embedding (OLE) technologies. It allows developers to create reusable software components that can interact with multiple applications on a Windows computer. ActiveX controls are one such component, which can be embedded in web pages to provide functionality such as multimedia playback, interactive page elements, and even entire applications.

For example, an ActiveX control could be used to create a calendar widget on a webpage. This widget could allow users to select dates, view events, and perform other calendar-related tasks directly within the webpage. The ActiveX control would be written in a language like C++ or Visual Basic, and would be packaged as a .ocx file. This file could then be embedded in the webpage using the **<object>** HTML tag.

However, it's important to note that ActiveX has largely been phased out in favor of more modern and secure technologies. Most modern web browsers, including Microsoft's own Edge browser, no longer support ActiveX controls due to security concerns. While ActiveX controls can still be used in certain contexts, such as in desktop applications or in Internet Explorer, their use is generally discouraged for new development.

Game Development: The Case of Doom

Doom, developed by id Software and released in 1993, is one of the most influential video games in history. It popularized the first-person shooter genre and introduced many technical innovations that have since become standard in game development.

Doom was written in C, a language that provides a good balance between high-level abstraction and low-level control over the hardware. This allowed the developers to create a game that was both complex and highly performant, even on the relatively limited hardware of the time.

One of the key technical innovations in Doom was its graphics engine. Unlike earlier games, which used a top-down or side-scrolling perspective, Doom presented the game world from the player's first-person perspective. This was achieved using a technique called raycasting, which involves casting rays from the player's position into the game world to determine what should be visible on the screen.

Another innovation in Doom was its networked multiplayer mode. Doom allowed up to four players to play together over a local area network (LAN), which was a novel feature at the time. This was achieved using a peer-to-peer networking model, where each player's computer would send updates to and receive updates from all the other players' computers.

Chapter 5: Database Management with C++

Understanding How to Interact with Databases Using C++

Understanding how to work with databases in C++ is essential for developing robust and efficient applications that require persistent storage and retrieval of data.

Connecting to Databases

The first step in database management with C++ is establishing a connection to the database. C++ provides libraries and APIs, such as ODBC (Open Database Connectivity) and JDBC (Java Database Connectivity), that allow developers to connect to a wide range of databases, including popular ones like MySQL, SQLite, PostgreSQL, and Oracle. These libraries provide functions and classes to handle connection parameters, authentication, and establish a secure connection to the database server.

Executing SQL Queries

Once connected, C++ enables developers to execute SQL (Structured Query Language) queries against the database. SQL is a standard language used for managing and manipulating relational databases. With C++, developers can build and execute SQL queries to perform operations such as retrieving data (SELECT), inserting records (INSERT), updating existing data (UPDATE), and deleting records (DELETE). C++ libraries provide methods and classes to construct SQL queries, bind parameters, execute them, and retrieve results.

Database Operations and Transactions

C++ facilitates various database operations beyond basic CRUD (Create, Read, Update, Delete) operations. Developers can perform advanced tasks such as creating and modifying database schemas, defining table relationships, indexing, and implementing complex queries involving joins and aggregations. Additionally, C++ supports transaction management to ensure data integrity and consistency. Developers can initiate transactions, commit changes, or roll back the transaction in case of errors or failures.

Data Mapping and Object-Relational Mapping (ORM)

C++ offers the flexibility to map database entities to C++ objects, enabling developers to work with databases using an object-oriented approach. Object-Relational Mapping (ORM) libraries, like ODB and Qt's Object-Relational Mapping (Qt ORM), provide tools and frameworks to simplify the mapping process and handle database operations transparently. ORM frameworks help abstract the complexities of database interaction, allowing developers to focus on business logic and working with objects instead of writing low-level database code.

Performance Optimization and Security

Efficient database management in C++ involves performance optimization techniques. Developers can optimize database operations by using prepared statements, stored procedures, and optimizing query execution plans. Additionally, C++ provides mechanisms for securing database interactions, such as parameterized queries, input validation, and encryption techniques, to prevent SQL injection attacks and ensure data confidentiality.

Practical Examples of C++ Database Management

Database management is a crucial aspect of many software applications. C++ does not have built-in support for database management, but there are several libraries available that provide this functionality. These libraries allow you to interact with databases using SQL, a standard language for managing data in a relational database.

One such library is SQLite, a C library that provides a lightweight disk-based database. SQLite doesn't require a separate server process and allows accessing the database using a nonstandard variant of the SQL query language. Some applications can use SQLite for internal data storage.

Another library is SOCI, often called "The C++ Database Access Library". SOCI is a database access library for C++ that makes the illusion of embedding SQL queries in the regular C++ code, staying entirely within the Standard C++.

Let's explore how we can use these libraries to manage a database in a C++ application.

SQLite with C++

SQLite is a C library, but it can be used in a C++ program. Here's an example of how you might use SQLite to create a database, create a table, and insert some data:

```cpp
#include <sqlite3.h>
#include <string>
#include <iostream>

int main() {
    sqlite3* DB;
    int exit = 0;
    exit = sqlite3_open("example.db", &DB);
    std::string sql = "CREATE TABLE PERSON("
            "ID INT PRIMARY KEY     NOT NULL, "
            "NAME          TEXT    NOT NULL, "
            "SURNAME        TEXT     NOT NULL, "
            "AGE          INT     NOT NULL, "
            "ADDRESS        CHAR(50), "
            "SALARY        REAL );";
    char* messageError;
    exit = sqlite3_exec(DB, sql.c_str(), NULL, 0, &messageError);
    if (exit != SQLITE_OK) {
        std::cerr << "Error Create Table" << std::endl;
        sqlite3_free(messageError);
    }
    else
        std::cout << "Table created Successfully" << std::endl;
    sqlite3_close(DB);
    return (0);
}
```

In this example, we first open a connection to the database using **sqlite3_open()**. We then define a SQL query to create a table. We execute the query using **sqlite3_exec()**. If the query execution is not successful, we print an error message. Finally, we close the connection to the database using **sqlite3_close()**.

SOCI with C++

SOCI provides a more C++-like interface for database access. Here's an example of how you might use SOCI to interact with a PostgreSQL database:

```cpp
#include <soci/soci.h>

#include <soci/postgresql/soci-postgresql.h>

#include <iostream>

#include <istream>

#include <ostream>

#include <string>

#include <exception>


using namespace soci;


int main()

{

    try

    {

        session sql(postgresql, "dbname=mydb user=myuser password=mypass");


        int count;

        sql << "SELECT COUNT(*) FROM mytable", into(count);


        std::cout << "We have " << count << " entries in the table. \n";


        std::string name;
```

```
    sql << "SELECT name FROM mytable WHERE id = 1", into(name);


    std::cout << "The first entry is " << name << '\n';
  }
catch (std::exception const & e)
  {
    std::cerr << "Error: " << e.what() << '\n';
  }


  return 0;
}
```

In this example, we first create a **session** object, which represents a connection to the database. We then execute SQL queries using the **<<** operator. We use the **into()** function to retrieve the result of a query. If any error occurs, we catch it and print an error message.

Chapter 6: C++ in Industrial IoT and Microcontroller Firmware

The Importance of C++ in Industrial IoT Projects and Microcontroller Firmware

We will explore how C++ serves as a powerful programming language in these domains and the advantages it offers for building robust and efficient applications for IoT devices and microcontrollers.

Efficient Resource Utilization

C++ is known for its ability to optimize resource utilization, making it an ideal choice for industrial IoT projects and microcontroller firmware. These applications often run on devices with limited resources such as memory and processing power. C++ allows developers to write code that maximizes performance and minimizes resource consumption, ensuring efficient utilization of system resources.

Low-Level Hardware Access

Industrial IoT projects and microcontroller firmware often require direct access to hardware components for tasks like sensor interfacing, control system integration, and data acquisition. C++ enables low-level programming and provides mechanisms for accessing and manipulating hardware resources directly. This level of control is crucial in ensuring precise and reliable communication with devices and peripherals in industrial environments.

Real-Time Responsiveness

Many industrial IoT applications and microcontroller firmware operate in real-time environments where responsiveness is critical. C++ supports deterministic behavior and allows developers to write code with predictable execution times. This makes it possible to meet strict timing requirements and ensure timely response to critical events, such as sensor data processing or control system updates.

Safety and Reliability

In industrial settings, safety and reliability are of utmost importance. C++ offers features like strong type checking, exception handling, and support for design patterns that contribute to writing robust and error-free code. These features are essential for ensuring the safe operation of industrial IoT systems and microcontroller firmware.

Exploring Examples of C++ Usage in ARM-based IoT Devices like Raspberry Pi

ARM-based devices, such as the Raspberry Pi, have become popular platforms for IoT development due to their low cost, low power consumption, and high performance.

C++ is a versatile language that is well-suited to IoT development on these devices. Its efficiency and low-level capabilities make it ideal for working with hardware, while its object-oriented features make it powerful and flexible for higher-level software development.

Let's explore some examples of how C++ can be used in IoT applications on ARM-based devices like the Raspberry Pi.

Interfacing with Hardware

One of the key aspects of IoT development is interfacing with hardware. This could include sensors (like temperature or humidity sensors), actuators (like motors or LEDs), or communication devices (like WiFi or Bluetooth modules).

C++ can interface with this hardware through the device's GPIO (General Purpose Input/Output) pins. Libraries like WiringPi and pigpio provide a C++ interface to the Raspberry Pi's GPIO pins, allowing you to read from and write to these pins.

For example, you could use C++ and the WiringPi library to blink an LED connected to a GPIO pin on the Raspberry Pi:

```
#include <wiringPi.h>
#include <iostream>


int main() {
    wiringPiSetup();
    pinMode(0, OUTPUT);


    for (int i = 0; i < 10; i++) {
        digitalWrite(0, HIGH);
        delay(500);
        digitalWrite(0, LOW);
        delay(500);
    }


    return 0;
}
```

In this example, we first initialize the WiringPi library with **wiringPiSetup**(). We then set GPIO pin 0 (which corresponds to physical pin 11 on the Raspberry Pi) to output mode with **pinMode**(). We then enter a loop where we turn the LED on and off every half second with **digitalWrite**(), using **delay**() to pause between state changes.

Networking and Communication

Many IoT applications involve some form of networking or communication, whether it's sending data to a remote server, receiving commands from a user, or communicating with other IoT devices.

C++ provides several libraries for networking and communication, such as Boost.Asio for asynchronous networking, libcurl for HTTP requests, and MQTT-C for MQTT, a lightweight messaging protocol commonly used in IoT applications.

For example, you could use C++ and the libcurl library to send a HTTP GET request to a remote server:

```
#include <curl/curl.h>
#include <iostream>


int main() {
    CURL* curl = curl_easy_init();
    if(curl) {
        CURLcode res;
        curl_easy_setopt(curl, CURLOPT_URL, "http://example.com");
        res = curl_easy_perform(curl);
        if(res != CURLE_OK)
            std::cerr << "curl_easy_perform() failed: " << curl_easy_strerror(res) << std::endl;
        curl_easy_cleanup(curl);
    }
    return 0;
}
```

In this example, we first initialize a CURL handle with **curl_easy_init**(). We then set the URL to request with **curl_easy_setopt**(), and perform the request with **curl_easy_perform**(). If the request fails, we print an error message. Finally, we clean up the CURL handle with **curl_easy_cleanup**().

Multithreading and Concurrency

Many IoT applications need to perform multiple tasks at the same time. For example, an IoT device might need to read sensor data, control actuators, and communicate with a remote server all at the same time.

C++ provides several features for multithreading and concurrency, such as the **<thread>** and **<future>** libraries introduced in C++11. These libraries allow you to easily create and manage threads, and to perform tasks asynchronously.

For example, you could use C++ and the **<thread>** library to blink an LED in a separate thread:

```cpp
#include <wiringPi.h>
#include <thread>
#include <chrono>


void blink() {
    pinMode(0, OUTPUT);
    for (int i = 0; i < 10; i++) {
        digitalWrite(0, HIGH);
        std::this_thread::sleep_for(std::chrono::milliseconds(500));
        digitalWrite(0, LOW);
        std::this_thread::sleep_for(std::chrono::milliseconds(500));
    }
}


int main() {
    wiringPiSetup();
    std::thread blinkThread(blink);
    blinkThread.join();
    return 0;
}
```

In this example, we first define a **blink()** function that blinks an LED. We then create a new thread with **std::thread** that runs this function. We wait for the thread to finish with **join()** before exiting the program.

Chapter 7: Practical C++ Projects

Advanced Projects that Showcase the Use of C++ in Various Applications

These projects will showcase the practical application of complex structures and database management concepts in real-world scenarios. By working on these projects, readers will gain hands-on experience and further enhance their skills in C++ programming.

Game Engine Development

Building a game engine from scratch is a challenging project that can showcase many aspects of C++. This could include rendering graphics with a library like OpenGL or DirectX, handling user input, managing game physics, and more. You could start by building a simple 2D game engine, and then expand it to support 3D graphics, advanced physics, and other features.

Financial Trading System

Financial institutions often use C++ for high-frequency trading systems due to its performance characteristics. You could build a simulated trading system that uses real-time market data to make trading decisions. This could involve complex algorithms, multithreaded programming, networking, and more.

Machine Learning Library

While Python is often used for machine learning, C++ can be used to implement the underlying algorithms for performance reasons. You could build a library that implements common machine learning algorithms, like linear regression, k-means clustering, or neural networks. This would involve a lot of math and possibly some parallel programming.

Internet of Things (IoT) Device

With a Raspberry Pi or similar device, you could build an IoT device that uses sensors to collect data, and then sends that data to a server for processing. This could involve interfacing with hardware, networking, multithreaded programming, and more. For example, you could build a weather station that collects data from various sensors and sends it to a server for analysis and visualization.

Database Management System

Building a simple database management system (DBMS) can be a great way to understand how databases work under the hood. This could involve data structures, algorithms, file I/O, and possibly networking if you want to support remote connections. You could start by building a simple in-memory database, and then expand it to support disk storage, SQL queries, and other features.

Ray Tracer

A ray tracer is a program that generates images by tracing the path of light through pixels in an image plane. Building a ray tracer can be a great way to learn about computer graphics, algorithms, and performance optimization in C++. You could start by building a simple ray tracer that supports spheres and planes, and then expand it to support complex 3D models, advanced lighting and shading, and other features.

Detailed Guides for Project Development using Advanced C++ Features

These features make C++ suitable for a variety of projects, from operating systems and game engines to web servers and machine learning libraries. In this guide, we'll explore how to use advanced C++ features in project development.

Object-Oriented Programming (OOP)

OOP is a programming paradigm that uses "objects" – instances of classes – which are capable of containing data and methods that manipulate that data. C++ supports the four fundamental principles of OOP: encapsulation, inheritance, polymorphism, and abstraction.

For example, if you're developing a game, you might have a **Player** class with data members for the player's name, score, and position, and methods to move the player, update the score, etc. You could then create instances of this class for each player in the game.

Templates

Templates allow you to write generic code that works with different data types. They can be used to create function templates and class templates.

For instance, if you're developing a data structure library, you might use templates to create a generic **Array** class that can hold elements of any type.

```
template <typename T>
class Array {
    T* arr;
    int size;
public:
    Array(T arr[], int s);
    void print();
};
```

Standard Template Library (STL)

The STL is a powerful library that provides several generic classes and functions, which includes collections of algorithms, containers, iterators, and more.

For example, if you're developing a text processing tool, you might use the **std::string** class for text manipulation, **std::vector** or **std::map** for storing data, and algorithms like **std::sort** or **std::find** for processing data.

Exception Handling

Exception handling is a mechanism for handling both hardware and software errors. C++ provides several keywords for this, including **try**, **catch**, **throw**, and **noexcept**.

For instance, if you're developing a financial application, you might use exception handling to ensure that transactions are processed correctly, and to handle any errors that occur.

Multithreading

Multithreading is a specialized form of multitasking that allows multiple threads of execution within a single process. C++11 introduced the **<thread>** library to support multithreading.

For example, if you're developing a web server, you might use multithreading to handle multiple client connections simultaneously.

Smart Pointers

Smart pointers are a feature of C++ that provides automatic memory management, which helps in preventing memory leaks. They are objects that behave like pointers, but also have additional features like automatic memory management.

For instance, if you're developing a large-scale application where memory management is crucial, you might use smart pointers like **std::unique_ptr**, **std::shared_ptr**, or **std::weak_ptr** to manage resources.

Lambda Expressions

Lambda expressions are a feature introduced in C++11 that allow you to write anonymous functions directly in your code. They are particularly useful when working with template functions like **std::sort** or **std::for_each**.

For example, if you're developing a graphics application, you might use lambda expressions to define custom sorting or drawing routines.

Move Semantics and Rvalue References

Move semantics is a feature introduced in C++11 that allows resources to be moved, rather than copied, between objects. This can significantly improve performance for large objects.

For instance, if you're developing a 3D modeling application, you might use move semantics to efficiently handle large amounts of vertex and texture data.

Chapter 8: The Future with C++

Exploring Future Trends in C++

C++ has been a staple in the programming world for decades, and it continues to evolve and adapt to the needs of developers. Here are some trends that are likely to shape the future of C++:

C++20 and Beyond

The C++20 standard was finalized in 2020 and introduced several new features and improvements, such as modules, coroutines, concepts, ranges, and more. These features aim to make C++ more powerful, easier to use, and more efficient.

Looking ahead, the C++ committee is already working on the next versions of the standard, C++23 and beyond. While it's too early to say exactly what these versions will include, it's likely that they will continue to improve on the features introduced in C++20, as well as introduce new features to address the needs of modern software development.

Concurrency and Parallelism

As hardware continues to evolve, with multi-core and many-core processors becoming increasingly common, there is a growing need for languages that can effectively handle concurrency and parallelism. C++ has been adding features to better support these paradigms, such as the **<thread>** and **<future>** libraries in C++11, and the parallel algorithms in C++17.

In the future, we can expect C++ to continue to improve its support for concurrency and parallelism, making it easier for developers to write code that can take full advantage of modern hardware.

Safety and Security

As software becomes increasingly complex and interconnected, safety and security are becoming more important than ever. C++ has a reputation for being a "sharp tool" that gives developers a lot of power, but also a lot of responsibility.

In recent years, there has been a push to make C++ safer and more secure, by discouraging unsafe practices, improving support for static analysis tools, and introducing safer alternatives to traditional C++ features. This trend is likely to continue in the future, as the C++ community continues to balance the need for power and performance with the need for safety and security.

Interoperability

C++ is often used in conjunction with other languages, such as C, Python, and JavaScript. As such, there is a growing need for better interoperability between C++ and other languages.

This could involve improving the C++ Foreign Function Interface (FFI), which allows C++ code to call functions written in other languages and vice versa, or developing better tools and libraries for binding C++ code to other languages.

Tooling

While C++ has a wealth of libraries and frameworks, its tooling has traditionally lagged behind other languages. However, this has been improving in recent years, with the development of more powerful IDEs, better package managers, and more comprehensive testing and profiling tools.

In the future, we can expect the C++ tooling ecosystem to continue to improve, making it easier for developers to write, test, debug, and deploy C++ code.

Advice on Staying Up-to-Date with the Latest C++ Developments

Staying up-to-date with the latest developments in C++ is crucial for any developer working with the language. Here are some strategies to help you keep abreast of the latest changes and trends in C++:

1. Follow the Standards Committee

The ISO C++ Standards Committee (also known as WG21) is responsible for the development of the C++ language standard. The committee's papers and meeting reports are publicly available and provide a wealth of information about the current state and future direction of C++. You can find these documents on the official ISO C++ website.

2. Read C++ Blogs and Websites

There are many blogs and websites dedicated to C++ that regularly publish articles on the latest features, best practices, and advanced techniques. Some notable ones include:

- isocpp.org: The official website of the Standard C++ Foundation, which posts news and resources about C++.

- cppreference.com: A wiki that documents the entire C++ language and standard library.

- The blogs of C++ experts like Herb Sutter, Bjarne Stroustrup, and Scott Meyers.

3. Attend Conferences and Meetups

Conferences like CppCon, Meeting C++, and C++Now, among others, are great opportunities to learn from and network with other C++ professionals. Many of these conferences also make their talks available online for free.

Local C++ meetups can also be a good way to stay informed and meet other developers in your area. You can find meetups on websites like Meetup.com.

4. Participate in Online Communities

Online communities like Stack Overflow, the C++ subreddit, and the C++ sections of Quora and Hacker News are places where you can ask questions, share knowledge, and learn from other developers.

5. Take Online Courses and Tutorials

Online learning platforms like Coursera, Udemy, and Pluralsight offer courses on C++, including courses on the latest features of C++20. YouTube also has many tutorials and lecture series on C++.

6. Read Books

There are many books that cover advanced C++ topics and the latest features of C++20. Some notable ones include "A Tour of C++" by Bjarne Stroustrup, "Effective Modern C++" by Scott Meyers, and "C++ Concurrency in Action" by Anthony Williams.

7. Practice Coding

Finally, the best way to stay up-to-date with C++ is to use it regularly. Try to use the latest features and techniques in your projects, and don't be afraid to experiment and learn by doing.

Book 6 - C# and C++: Bridging the Gap

Introduction: The Power of C# and C++ Together

Welcome to "C# and C++: Bridging the Gap," a comprehensive guide that explores the synergies between two of the most powerful programming languages in the software industry. This book is designed to provide you with a deep understanding of both languages and how they can be used together to create robust, high-performance applications.

C# and C++ each have their strengths and are suited to different types of tasks. C++, with its low-level capabilities and high efficiency, is often the language of choice for system programming, game development, and other applications where performance is paramount. On the other hand, C#, with its simpler syntax and extensive library support, is commonly used for enterprise software, web applications, and mobile development.

However, the true power of these languages is realized when they are used together. By leveraging the strengths of both languages, developers can create applications that are not only powerful and efficient, but also easy to develop and maintain. This is where the concept of interoperability comes into play, allowing C# and C++ to work together seamlessly.

This book will guide you through the process of combining C# and C++, from understanding the basics of interoperability, to performing complex data analysis, to building high-performance applications. You will learn not only the theory behind these concepts, but also how to apply them in practical, real-world situations.

In Chapter 1, we will explore the techniques for interoperation between C# and C++. This includes understanding the commonalities and differences between the two languages, and how to use each language's features to your advantage. We will also provide practical examples and use cases of C# and C++ interoperability, giving you a solid foundation to build upon.

In Chapter 2, we will delve into the role of C# and C++ in data analysis, and how they can be used together to create powerful data analysis tools. This includes a detailed guide on creating these tools, from understanding the data, to processing it, to visualizing the results.

In Chapter 3, we will discuss techniques and best practices for building high-performance applications using C# and C++. This includes understanding the performance characteristics of both languages, how to optimize your code for performance, and case studies of high-performance applications.

In Chapter 4, we will provide hands-on C# and C++ projects that allow you to apply what you've learned in a practical context. Each project includes a detailed walkthrough, including the objectives of the project and the solutions to any challenges you might encounter.

Finally, in Chapter 5, we will explore how C# and C++ fit into the broader programming ecosystem. This includes understanding how these languages interact with other technologies, and how to continue your learning and development in C# and C++.

By the end of this book, you will have a deep understanding of both C# and C++, and how to use these languages together to create powerful applications. Whether you're a seasoned developer looking to expand your skill set, or a beginner eager to dive into the world of programming, this book will provide you with the knowledge and skills you need to succeed. So, let's get started on this exciting journey of bridging the gap between C# and C++.

Chapter 1: Interoperability between C# and C++

Exploring the Techniques for Interoperation between C# and C++

Interoperability between C# and C++ is a crucial aspect when you're working on a project that requires the strengths of both languages. C# is a high-level language that excels in rapid application development, while C++ is a lower-level language that provides greater control over system resources. Here are some techniques for achieving interoperation between these two powerful languages:

Platform Invocation Services (P/Invoke)

P/Invoke is a technology in .NET that allows managed code (like C#) to call unmanaged functions implemented in a DLL written in a language like C or C++. This is especially useful when you have legacy C++ code that you want to use in a C# application.

Here's an example of how you might use P/Invoke in C# to call a C++ function:

```
// C++ code
extern "C" __declspec(dllexport) int Add(int a, int b)
{
    return a + b;
}


// C# code
class Program
{
```

```
[DllImport("MyLibrary.dll")]
public static extern int Add(int a, int b);


static void Main()
{
    Console.WriteLine(Add(2, 3));  // Outputs: 5
}
}
```

In this example, the C++ function **Add** is declared with **extern "C"** to prevent name mangling, and **__declspec(dllexport)** to export it from the DLL. In the C# code, the **Add** function is declared with the **DllImport** attribute, specifying the name of the DLL, and then it can be called like any other C# function.

C++/CLI

C++/CLI is a language specification created by Microsoft that allows C++ programs to use .NET features. It's a bridge between C++ and .NET, allowing code written in each to interact with each other more seamlessly than with P/Invoke.

Here's an example of how you might use C++/CLI to call a C# method from C++:

```
// C# code
namespace MyNamespace
{
    public class MyClass
    {
        public int Add(int a, int b)
        {
            return a + b;
        }
    }
}
```

```cpp
// C++ code
using namespace MyNamespace;


int main()
{
    MyClass^ myClass = gcnew MyClass();
    int result = myClass->Add(2, 3);
    Console::WriteLine(result);  // Outputs: 5
}
```

In this example, the C# method **Add** is part of the **MyClass** class in the **MyNamespace** namespace. In the C++/CLI code, a **MyClass** object is created with **gcnew**, and then the **Add** method can be called on this object.

COM Interop

COM (Component Object Model) Interop is a technology that allows .NET code to interact with COM objects, which can be written in a language like C++. This is a more complex method of interoperation, but it allows for a high degree of control and flexibility.

Practical Examples and Use Cases of C# and C++ Interoperability

Interoperability between C# and C++ can be incredibly useful in a variety of scenarios. Here are some practical examples and use cases:

Using Legacy C++ Libraries in a C# Application

Suppose you have a legacy C++ library that performs some complex calculations. Rewriting the entire library in C# could be time-consuming and error-prone. Instead, you can use P/Invoke to call the C++ functions from your C# code.

```cpp
// C++ code in MyMathLibrary.dll
extern "C" __declspec(dllexport) double CalculateSomethingComplex(double a, double b)
{
```

```
    // Some complex calculation...

}


// C# code

class Program

{

    [DllImport("MyMathLibrary.dll")]

    public static extern double CalculateSomethingComplex(double a, double b);


    static void Main()

    {

        double result = CalculateSomethingComplex(2.5, 3.5);

        Console.WriteLine(result);

    }

}
```

Creating a High-Performance C# Application with C++ Components

C# is great for rapid application development, but for performance-critical code, C++ often has the edge. You can write the performance-critical parts of your application in C++, and then use C++/CLI to bridge the gap between the C++ and C# components.

```
// C++/CLI code in MyPerformanceLibrary.dll

public ref class PerformanceClass

{

public:

    static double PerformanceCriticalFunction(double a, double b)

    {

        // Some performance-critical operation...

    }

};
```

```csharp
// C# code
class Program
{
    static void Main()
    {
        double result = MyPerformanceLibrary.PerformanceClass.PerformanceCriticalFunction(2.5, 3.5);
        Console.WriteLine(result);
    }
}
```

In all these examples, the key is to play to the strengths of each language: use C# for rapid application development and high-level features, and use C++ for performance-critical code and low-level features. By doing so, you can create applications that are both powerful and efficient.

Chapter 2: Data Analysis with C# and C++

The Role of C# and C++ in Data Analysis and How They Can Be Used Together

Data analysis plays a crucial role in various domains, including scientific research, business intelligence, finance, and healthcare. C# and C++ are two powerful programming languages that can be effectively utilized for data analysis tasks. In this chapter, we will explore the role of C# and C++ in data analysis and how they can be combined to leverage their respective strengths.

C# in Data Analysis

C# is a high-level, object-oriented programming language known for its simplicity, versatility, and extensive library support. When it comes to data analysis, C# provides a rich set of tools and frameworks that enable efficient data processing, manipulation, and visualization. Some key aspects of using C# in data analysis include:

- Language Features: C# offers a range of features that facilitate data handling, such as powerful data structures (e.g., lists, dictionaries) and LINQ (Language-Integrated Query) for querying and manipulating data.

- Libraries and Frameworks: C# boasts numerous libraries and frameworks tailored for data analysis, such as Microsoft's .NET Framework, ADO.NET for database access, and popular third-party libraries like Math.NET Numerics and Accord.NET.

- Visualization: C# provides robust graphical capabilities through libraries like Windows Presentation Foundation (WPF) and Windows Forms, enabling developers to create interactive data visualizations and dashboards.

C++ in Data Analysis

C++ is a lower-level, performance-oriented programming language widely known for its efficiency and direct hardware access. Although C++ requires more manual memory management and offers a steeper learning curve, it excels in computationally intensive tasks and provides fine-grained control over system resources. In data analysis, C++ is often utilized for:

- Numerical Computing: C++ provides extensive support for numerical computing through libraries like Eigen, Armadillo, and Intel MKL. These libraries offer optimized algorithms for linear algebra, statistical analysis, and numerical simulations.

- Performance Optimization: C++ allows developers to fine-tune algorithms and leverage hardware-specific features, making it ideal for performance-critical applications that require real-time analysis or handle large datasets.

- Integration with Existing C++ Codebases: Many legacy systems and scientific libraries are written in C++, and integrating them with newer data analysis projects can be beneficial. C++ provides a seamless way to utilize these existing codebases, leveraging their functionality and performance advantages.

Bridging C# and C++ for Data Analysis

The combination of C# and C++ can be powerful for data analysis tasks, as it allows developers to capitalize on the strengths of both languages. Some common scenarios where C# and C++ can be effectively used together in data analysis include:

- Interoperability: C# and C++ can communicate with each other through mechanisms like PInvoke, COM Interop, or building C++/CLI wrappers. This enables seamless integration of C++ libraries or components into C# applications, leveraging the performance benefits of C++ while enjoying the productivity of C#.

- Algorithm Design and Implementation: C# can be used for rapid prototyping and algorithm design, while computationally intensive or performance-critical portions of the code can be implemented in C++ for optimal execution speed.

- Multithreading and Parallel Computing: C++ provides fine-grained control over multithreading and parallel execution, making it well-suited for performance optimization in data-intensive applications. By combining C#'s ease of use with C++'s parallel programming capabilities, developers can achieve efficient utilization of system resources.

Detailed Guide on Creating Data Analysis Tools with C# and C++

Data analysis plays a vital role in today's data-driven world, and having the right tools is essential for extracting insights and making informed decisions. C# and C++ are two powerful programming languages that, when combined, can create robust and efficient data analysis tools. In this chapter, we will provide a detailed guide on creating data analysis tools using C# and C++, covering the key steps, techniques, and best practices.

Designing the Data Analysis Tool

The first step in creating a data analysis tool is to define its purpose and functionality. This involves understanding the specific requirements of the analysis task and identifying the necessary features. Some common functionalities of data analysis tools include data importing and preprocessing, statistical analysis, data visualization, and report generation. By clearly defining the objectives, you can better plan the architecture and design of the tool.

Leveraging C# for Rapid Development

C# provides a high-level, object-oriented programming environment that promotes rapid development and productivity. When creating a data analysis tool, C# can be leveraged for tasks such as:

- User Interface: C# offers intuitive and feature-rich frameworks like Windows Presentation Foundation (WPF) or Windows Forms to create user-friendly interfaces for data input, parameter configuration, and result visualization.

- Data Handling and Analysis: C# provides extensive support for data manipulation, processing, and analysis. Utilizing libraries such as LINQ (Language-Integrated Query) and Math.NET Numerics, you can perform operations like filtering, aggregating, and transforming data with ease.

- Visualization: C# libraries like Microsoft Chart Controls or third-party libraries such as Plotly.NET and OxyPlot enable the creation of visually appealing and interactive charts, graphs, and other visual representations of data.

Harnessing C++ for Performance-Intensive Tasks

While C# is well-suited for rapid development and data handling, certain data analysis tasks may require performance optimizations. This is where C++ shines. Consider using C++ for:

- Algorithm Optimization: Implementing computationally intensive algorithms or complex mathematical calculations in C++ can significantly improve performance. C++ offers low-level control, manual memory management, and efficient use of hardware resources.

- Integrating Existing C++ Libraries: If you have established C++ libraries or components for specific data analysis tasks, you can integrate them seamlessly into your C# application using techniques like PInvoke or COM Interop.

- Multithreading and Parallel Computing: C++ provides fine-grained control over multithreading and parallel execution, which can be advantageous for data-intensive tasks that can benefit from parallelization.

Ensuring Interoperability Between C# and C++

To effectively bridge C# and C++ in your data analysis tool, it is crucial to establish interoperability between the two languages. Techniques like Platform Invocation Services (PInvoke), COM Interop, or building C++/CLI wrappers can facilitate seamless communication and integration. This allows you to leverage the performance benefits of C++ while leveraging the productivity and rich ecosystem of C#.

Testing and Debugging

As with any software development project, thorough testing and debugging are crucial for ensuring the reliability and accuracy of your data analysis tool. Use appropriate testing frameworks and methodologies to validate the functionality and handle various scenarios and edge cases. Debugging tools and techniques specific to C# and C++ can help identify and fix any issues that may arise during development.

Deployment and Distribution

Once your data analysis tool is ready, consider the deployment and distribution process. Depending on the requirements, you can choose to distribute the tool as a standalone executable, a web application, or integrate it into an existing software ecosystem. Consider packaging and deployment options, such as ClickOnce deployment or containerization, to ensure smooth installation and usage for end-users.

Chapter 3: Building High-Performance Applications with C# and C++

Techniques and Best Practices for Building High-Performance Applications using C# and C++

In today's technology landscape, building high-performance applications is essential for delivering fast and responsive software solutions. C# and C++ are two powerful languages that, when used together, can unlock the potential for creating high-performance applications that combine the productivity and ease of development of C# with the performance optimizations of C++. In this chapter, we will explore various techniques and best practices for building high-performance applications using C# and C++.

Before diving into the implementation, it is crucial to have a clear understanding of the performance requirements of your application. Identify the critical areas that require optimization, such as computational-intensive algorithms, memory management, or data processing.

Leverage C# for Productivity and High-Level Abstractions

C# provides a high-level, managed environment that promotes productivity and ease of development. Utilize the following techniques to enhance performance in your C# code:

- Efficient Data Structures and Algorithms: Choose appropriate data structures and algorithms that minimize computational complexity. Utilize built-in collections and algorithms from the .NET framework, such as the List<T> or Dictionary<TKey, TValue> classes, to improve performance.

- Asynchronous Programming: Take advantage of asynchronous programming features in C# to create responsive applications. By using async/await keywords and the Task Parallel Library (TPL), you can improve resource utilization and responsiveness.

- Memory Management: Employ best practices for memory management, such as avoiding unnecessary object allocations, disposing of unmanaged resources, and utilizing object pooling when appropriate. The use of IDisposable and the using statement can help manage resource cleanup efficiently.

- Just-In-Time (JIT) Compilation: C# utilizes JIT compilation to convert IL code into native machine code at runtime. This dynamic compilation can improve performance by optimizing the execution of frequently used code paths.

Harness the Power of C++ for Performance-Critical Tasks

When performance is of utmost importance, integrating C++ code into your C# application can provide significant benefits. Consider the following techniques:

- Implement Performance-Critical Modules in C++: Identify performance-critical modules or algorithms and implement them in C++ for maximum efficiency. Use C++'s low-level control, manual memory management, and ability to interface with hardware resources to achieve optimal performance.

- Interoperability between C# and C++: Establish seamless interoperability between C# and C++ code to leverage the strengths of both languages. Techniques such as Platform Invocation Services (PInvoke), COM Interop, or building C++/CLI wrappers can facilitate smooth communication and integration.

Profiling and Performance Analysis

Profiling and performance analysis tools are essential for identifying bottlenecks and optimizing application performance. Utilize profiling tools specific to C# and C++, such as Visual Studio Profiler, to measure and analyze performance characteristics. These tools can help identify hotspots, memory leaks, excessive allocations, or inefficient algorithms, allowing you to optimize critical sections of your codebase.

Performance Testing and Benchmarking

Conduct thorough performance testing and benchmarking to validate the performance improvements achieved through optimization techniques. Establish performance metrics and compare different implementations to ensure that the desired performance gains are realized.

Continuous Improvement and Refactoring

Building high-performance applications is an ongoing process. Continuously monitor and analyze the performance of your application and proactively identify areas for improvement. Regular refactoring and code review can help identify and address performance issues, making your application more efficient over time.

Case Studies of High-Performance Applications

These case studies serve as practical examples to showcase the effectiveness of bridging the gap between these two languages in building high-performance applications. Let's delve into these case studies and see how C# and C++ have been leveraged to achieve impressive performance results.

Financial Trading System

Financial trading systems require low-latency and high-throughput processing to handle large volumes of real-time market data. By combining C# and C++, developers can create a system that benefits from the productivity and ease of development of C#, while harnessing the performance optimizations of C++. C# can be used for event handling, data aggregation, and business logic, while performance-critical components such as order matching algorithms or data parsing can be implemented in C++. This combination allows for optimal performance while maintaining the flexibility and rapid development cycle provided by C#.

Computer Graphics and Game Engines

Computer graphics and game engines demand real-time rendering, physics simulations, and efficient resource management. C++ has long been the language of choice for these domains due to its low-level control and ability to interact with hardware resources. However, C# can be employed for higher-level game logic, scripting, and user interface development. By using C++

for performance-critical components such as rendering pipelines or physics simulations, and utilizing C# for high-level scripting and gameplay systems, developers can create high-performance games and graphical applications.

Scientific Computing and Simulation

Scientific computing often involves complex calculations, simulations, and data processing. C++ provides the necessary performance optimizations for these computationally intensive tasks. By integrating C++ libraries or components into a C# application, developers can leverage the speed and efficiency of C++ for numerical computations, while using C# for data visualization, user interaction, and higher-level analysis. This combination allows scientists and engineers to benefit from the strengths of both languages and achieve high-performance scientific computing solutions.

Image and Video Processing

Image and video processing applications require efficient algorithms for tasks such as image manipulation, video compression, or real-time video processing. C++'s low-level control and ability to work with memory directly make it an ideal choice for implementing high-performance image and video processing routines. By integrating C++ modules into a C# application, developers can create powerful image and video processing pipelines while leveraging C#'s ease of use and rich ecosystem for tasks like user interface design and application integration.

Networking and Distributed Systems

Networking and distributed systems involve handling high-volume data transfers, managing network protocols, and ensuring efficient communication between distributed components. C++ can be used for implementing low-level networking protocols, socket programming, or optimizing data serialization and deserialization. C# can complement these components by providing higher-level abstractions, such as asynchronous programming models or frameworks for building distributed systems. This combination allows for the development of high-performance networking and distributed systems with efficient data processing and robust communication capabilities.

Chapter 4: C# and C++ Projects

Project-based Learning with Hands-on C# and C++ Projects

By engaging in practical projects, you will have the opportunity to apply your knowledge of both languages, reinforce concepts, and gain valuable experience in developing real-world applications. Let's explore the benefits of project-based learning and discover some inspiring C# and C++ projects to get you started.

Why Project-based Learning?

Project-based learning is an effective approach to learning programming languages like C# and C++. It offers numerous benefits that go beyond theoretical knowledge, providing a more immersive and engaging learning experience. Here are some advantages of project-based learning:

1. Application of Knowledge: Projects allow you to apply the concepts, principles, and techniques you have learned in a practical setting. This hands-on experience helps solidify your understanding and enhances your problem-solving skills.

2. Real-world Relevance: Projects mirror real-world scenarios, enabling you to develop solutions to common challenges faced in software development. This helps bridge the gap between theory and practice, preparing you for professional work.

3. Collaboration and Communication: Projects often involve teamwork, promoting collaboration and communication skills. Working with others fosters creativity, encourages sharing of ideas, and introduces you to industry best practices.

4. Self-directed Learning: Projects give you the freedom to explore topics of interest and pursue your own solutions. This autonomy fosters independent thinking, research, and resourcefulness.

Now, let's explore some exciting C# and C++ projects that you can undertake to enhance your skills and deepen your understanding of these languages.

Game Development

Embark on a game development project where you can utilize both C# and C++ to create engaging and interactive games. With C#, you can build the game logic, user interfaces, and scripting components, while C++ can be used for low-level performance optimizations, graphics rendering, or physics simulations. This project allows you to combine the best of both languages to develop a complete and immersive gaming experience.

Image Processing Application

Develop an image processing application that leverages the strengths of both C# and C++. Use C# for building the user interface, handling user interactions, and implementing high-level image processing algorithms. Utilize C++ for performance-critical operations like low-level image manipulation, implementing complex filters, or utilizing computer vision libraries. This project will deepen your understanding of image processing techniques while harnessing the performance advantages of C++.

Robotics Control System

Create a robotics control system that integrates C# and C++ to control and manage robotic devices. Use C# for designing the user interface, implementing high-level control algorithms, and handling real-time data visualization. Employ C++ for low-level hardware interactions, sensor data processing, or complex motion control algorithms. This project will expose you to the challenges and intricacies of robotics programming, combining the versatility of C# with the efficiency of C++.

Database Management Application

Develop a database management application that combines the features of C# and C++ to handle database operations efficiently. Use C# for designing the user interface, implementing business logic, and managing database connections. Utilize C++ to optimize performance-intensive tasks like data retrieval, indexing, or advanced data processing. This project will enhance your understanding of database management while utilizing the strengths of both languages.

Internet of Things (IoT) Project

Undertake an IoT project that integrates C# and C++ to create a smart and connected system. Use C# for building the cloud-based infrastructure, implementing web services, and developing user-friendly interfaces. Combine C++ for programming embedded devices, handling sensor data, or implementing real-time control algorithms. This project will expose you to the exciting world of IoT and demonstrate how C# and C++ can work together to create innovative solutions.

Detailed Walkthroughs of Each Project, Including Objectives and Solutions

By examining these projects, you will gain a deeper understanding of the integration of C# and C++, and how they can be leveraged to create powerful and efficient software solutions. Let's dive into the walkthroughs of the C# and C++ projects.

Project 1: Game Development

Objective

Develop an interactive game using C# and C++.

In this project, the goal is to create an engaging game by harnessing the strengths of both C# and C++. The primary objective is to design and implement game mechanics, user interfaces, and interactive elements using C#. Additionally, C++ can be utilized for performance optimizations, graphics rendering, or other computationally intensive tasks. By combining the two languages, you can create a game that seamlessly integrates high-level logic with low-level performance enhancements.

Solution

1. Design the game mechanics: Begin by outlining the game's rules, objectives, and mechanics. Use C# to implement the game logic, including character movements, collision detection, scoring systems, and level progression.

2. Create the user interface: Use C# to design and develop user-friendly interfaces for menus, settings, and game controls. Utilize C++ for rendering high-quality graphics, particle effects, or advanced visual elements.

3. Implement performance optimizations: Identify areas where performance improvements are required, such as complex physics simulations or AI algorithms. Utilize C++ to optimize these computationally intensive tasks, leveraging its lower-level control and memory management capabilities.

4. Test and refine: Continuously test the game, identifying bugs, and refining the gameplay experience. Pay attention to performance bottlenecks and optimize further as needed.

Project 2: Image Processing Application

Objective

Develop an image processing application that utilizes the capabilities of C# and C++.

This project focuses on leveraging C# and C++ to create an image processing application that combines high-level processing algorithms with low-level optimizations for performance-critical tasks.

Solution

1. Design the user interface: Use C# to design an intuitive user interface that allows users to load, manipulate, and save images. Implement functionalities such as cropping, resizing, filtering, and enhancing images using C#.

2. Implement high-level image processing algorithms: Utilize C# to implement high-level image processing algorithms, such as edge detection, image segmentation, or feature extraction.

3. Integrate low-level optimizations: Identify computationally intensive tasks that would benefit from lower-level optimizations. Utilize C++ to implement these optimizations, leveraging its control over memory management and CPU instructions.

4. Enhance performance: Benchmark the application and identify areas where further performance improvements are needed. Optimize critical sections of the code using C++ for better efficiency.

Project 3: Robotics Control System

Objective

Develop a robotics control system by combining the capabilities of C# and C++.

In this project, the aim is to create a control system for robotic devices, integrating C# for high-level control and C++ for low-level hardware interactions and performance-critical tasks.

Solution

1. Design the user interface: Use C# to design an intuitive user interface that allows users to control robotic devices, monitor sensor data, and visualize real-time feedback.

2. Implement high-level control algorithms: Utilize C# to implement control algorithms for various robotic tasks, such as motion planning, path following, or object detection.

3. Integrate low-level hardware interactions: Utilize C++ to interface with the robotic hardware, handle sensor data, and control actuators. Leverage the performance advantages of C++ to ensure real-time responsiveness and low latency.

4. Test and refine: Validate the control system by testing it with robotic devices, fine-tuning the algorithms, and ensuring reliable and precise control.

These project walkthroughs provide a glimpse into the objectives, challenges, and solutions involved in combining C# and C++ for practical applications. By following these detailed guides, you will gain hands-on experience and deepen your understanding of how to bridge the gap between C# and C++ effectively.

Chapter 5: Beyond C# and C++

Exploration of How C# and C++ Fit into the Broader Programming Ecosystem

While C# and C++ are powerful languages on their own, understanding their place and relevance in the larger context of programming can provide valuable insights into their capabilities and potential applications. Let's explore how C# and C++ interact with other programming languages, frameworks, and technologies.

Interoperability with Other Languages

C# and C++ offer interoperability with various programming languages, allowing developers to leverage their unique strengths in combination with other languages. For example, C# can seamlessly interoperate with languages like Python, Java, and JavaScript through libraries and frameworks like IronPython, JNI (Java Native Interface), and JavaScript interoperability in .NET Core. This interoperability opens up possibilities for combining the strengths of different languages to build robust and scalable applications.

Integration with Frameworks and Technologies

Both C# and C++ have extensive integration capabilities with popular frameworks and technologies. C# is closely tied to the .NET framework, providing access to a wide range of libraries and APIs for application development. It can be used with frameworks like ASP.NET for web development, Xamarin for cross-platform mobile app development, and Unity for game development. C++, on the other hand, is known for its compatibility with low-level systems programming, making it a natural choice for developing operating systems, embedded systems, and real-time applications.

Support for Multi-Platform Development

C# and C++ have evolved to support multi-platform development, enabling developers to create applications that can run on different operating systems and architectures. C# has the advantage of the .NET Core framework, which allows cross-platform development on Windows, macOS, and Linux. C++ has long been used for developing cross-platform applications, with its compilers and toolchains available on various platforms. By leveraging the portability of these languages, developers can reach a wider audience and ensure their applications run smoothly across different environments.

Integration with Existing Codebases

C# and C++ are often used in scenarios where integration with existing codebases is crucial. C# provides seamless integration with existing .NET codebases, allowing developers to leverage their investments in legacy applications or libraries. C++ offers compatibility with existing C codebases and libraries, making it a suitable choice for projects that require interfacing with established C-based systems or performance-critical tasks.

Support for Modern Development Practices

Both C# and C++ have adapted to modern development practices and paradigms. C# has embraced object-oriented programming (OOP), functional programming (FP), and asynchronous programming models, making it easier to write clean and maintainable code. C++ has evolved with features like modern C++ standards, smart pointers, and lambdas, enabling developers to write more expressive and efficient code. This adaptability allows developers to leverage the latest practices and patterns in their projects.

Preparing for Continued Learning and Development in C# and C++

As technology evolves and new advancements are made, it is crucial for developers to stay up-to-date with the latest trends and best practices in order to maximize their skills and effectiveness in using these programming languages. Let's explore some strategies and resources for continuous learning and development in C# and C++.

Stay Current with Language Updates

Both C# and C++ are continuously evolving, with new features and improvements being introduced in each language version. It is essential to stay informed about these updates to take advantage of new capabilities and enhance your programming skills. Follow official documentation, developer blogs, and community forums to stay up-to-date with language updates and learn about new features and techniques.

Explore Advanced Topics and Specializations

C# and C++ offer a wide range of advanced topics and specializations that you can explore to expand your knowledge and expertise. Consider delving into areas such as concurrency, parallel programming, memory management, design patterns, performance optimization, and software architecture. By diving deeper into these topics, you can gain a deeper understanding of the intricacies of these languages and unlock their full potential.

Engage in Community and Networking

Participating in developer communities and networking with other professionals is a valuable way to enhance your learning and development in C# and C++. Join online forums, attend conferences, and participate in local meetups to connect with like-minded individuals and exchange knowledge and experiences. Engaging in discussions, sharing your projects, and seeking feedback can provide valuable insights and help you grow as a developer.

Explore Open-Source Projects and Contributions

Contributing to open-source projects in C# and C++ is an excellent way to enhance your skills and gain practical experience. By working collaboratively with other developers on real-world projects, you can improve your understanding of best practices, coding standards, and teamwork. Additionally, exploring open-source projects allows you to learn from experienced developers and contribute to the community by sharing your own insights and code contributions.

Continuous Practice and Project Development

One of the most effective ways to improve your skills in C# and C++ is through continuous practice and project development. Regularly engage in coding exercises, challenges, and personal projects to reinforce your understanding of the languages and experiment with different techniques and approaches. Building practical applications and solving real-world problems will not only sharpen your coding skills but also provide you with a portfolio to showcase your abilities to potential employers or clients.

Explore Online Learning Platforms and Courses

Online learning platforms offer a wealth of resources, tutorials, and courses dedicated to C# and C++ programming. Platforms like Udemy, Coursera, and Pluralsight provide comprehensive courses taught by industry experts, covering various aspects of these languages. These courses offer structured learning paths, hands-on exercises, and practical examples to help you deepen your understanding and gain practical experience.

Book 7 - C# and C++: Career Preparation and Beyond

Introduction: Preparing for the Future

Welcome to "C# and C++: Career Preparation and Beyond," a comprehensive guide designed to equip you with the knowledge and skills needed to excel in your career as a C# and C++ developer. This book is more than just a technical manual; it's a roadmap to a successful career in the dynamic and rewarding field of programming.

Mastering C# and C++ can have a profound impact on your career. These languages are among the most widely used in the industry and offer a broad range of opportunities. Whether you're developing desktop applications, designing game engines, building enterprise systems, or creating cutting-edge AI algorithms, C# and C++ are tools that can help you achieve your goals.

In Chapter 1, we'll take a deep dive into the landscape of C# and C++ in the industry. We'll explore how these languages shape career opportunities and present research findings on their use across various sectors. This will give you a clear picture of where your skills can be applied and the potential paths your career can take.

Chapter 2 will guide you through the certifications and courses available for C# and C++. We'll discuss the importance of these certifications and how they can enhance your resume, helping you stand out in the competitive job market.

In Chapter 3, we'll review the essential skills required for proficient C# and C++ developers. This includes not only technical skills but also soft skills like problem-solving, communication, and teamwork. We'll also provide techniques for improving and mastering these skills.

Chapter 4 will provide an overview of the job market for C# and C++ developers. We'll offer tips for finding and applying to relevant jobs, and discuss how to navigate the job market to find opportunities that align with your career goals.

In Chapter 5, we'll delve into the art of resume building and interview preparation for C# and C++ developers. We'll share techniques for creating an impressive resume, performing well in interviews, and provide case studies and examples of successful interviews and resumes.

Chapter 6 will take you through the latest trends in the C# and C++ industries. We'll discuss the importance of staying current with updates and how to prepare for new advancements in these languages. This will ensure that you remain competitive and relevant in the ever-evolving tech industry.

Finally, in Chapter 7, we'll prepare you for continued self-learning and development in C# and C++. We'll provide resources and advice for ongoing development and learning, ensuring that you continue to grow and evolve as a programmer.

"C# and C++: Career Preparation and Beyond" is more than just a book; it's a stepping stone to a successful career in programming. By the end of this book, you'll have a clear understanding of where C# and C++ can take you, and the tools you need to get there. So, let's embark on this journey together, and prepare for the exciting future that lies ahead.

Chapter 1: Understanding the Landscape: Where C# and C++ are Used

Deep Dive into How Mastering C++ and C# Can Shape Your Career Opportunities

In today's technology-driven world, programming languages like C++ and C# play a significant role in shaping the career opportunities for aspiring developers. These two languages, each with its unique strengths, have gained immense popularity and found their application in various domains of the software industry. Mastering C++ and C# can open up a plethora of career paths and contribute to long-term professional success. In this chapter, we will delve into how acquiring proficiency in C++ and C# can impact your career trajectory and pave the way for exciting opportunities.

C++ is known for its performance and versatility, making it a preferred choice for developing high-performance applications and systems. From operating systems, game engines, and embedded systems to resource-intensive applications, C++ has a broad range of applications. Its usage extends to domains such as gaming, finance, automotive, aerospace, and more. By mastering C++, developers can become valuable assets in industries that require resource-efficient and reliable solutions. Additionally, proficiency in C++ can lead to career opportunities in firmware development, robotics, and other cutting-edge fields.

On the other hand, C# has established itself as a powerful language for building applications on the Microsoft .NET platform. C# is widely used for web development, desktop applications, mobile apps, and game development using the Unity game engine. Its ease of use, strong integration with the .NET framework, and managed memory allocation make it a popular choice for developing modern, scalable, and user-friendly applications. By mastering C#, developers can find opportunities in software development companies, IT consulting firms, and businesses that leverage Microsoft technologies.

Research Findings on the Use of C++ and C# in Various Industries

C++ and C# are two of the most widely used programming languages in the world, and their applications span across various industries. Recent research findings have shed light on how these languages are used, and the insights can be quite enlightening for both new and experienced developers.

In the software industry, C++ is often the language of choice for system software, game development, and real-time systems. Its efficiency and control over system resources make it ideal for applications where performance is paramount. For instance, many popular game engines, such as Unreal Engine, are built using C++. Similarly, operating systems like Windows and Linux have components written in C++.

On the other hand, C# is heavily used in enterprise software development. Its simplicity, along with the robust .NET framework, makes it a popular choice for business applications, web services, and desktop applications. For instance, many internal tools used by businesses are built with C#, and it's a common language for Windows desktop applications.

In the realm of web development, C# has carved out a significant niche with the ASP.NET framework, which is used to build dynamic websites and web applications. It's particularly popular in the enterprise space, where its combination of power and ease of use is highly valued.

In the growing field of data science and machine learning, both C++ and C# find their uses. C++ is often used for performance-intensive tasks, such as training large machine learning models, thanks to its efficiency. C#, with libraries like Accord.NET and CNTK, is also used for developing machine learning applications, especially in a .NET-centric environment.

In the hardware and embedded systems industry, C++ is commonly used due to its fine-grained control over hardware resources. It's used in the development of microcontroller programming, embedded systems, and for interfacing with hardware.

In the finance industry, both C++ and C# are used. C++ is used for high-frequency trading applications due to its speed, while C# is often used for building financial models, algorithms, and desktop applications.

In the education sector, C# is frequently used due to its readability and simplicity, making it a good language for teaching programming concepts. However, C++ is also taught, especially in courses focused on systems programming, game development, or where a deeper understanding of computer architecture is required.

Chapter 2: Certifications and Courses for C# and C++

Overview of Useful Certifications and Courses for Furthering Your Knowledge

In the ever-evolving world of programming, certifications and courses serve as valuable tools for enhancing your expertise and career prospects. This chapter explores some of the essential certifications and courses specifically tailored for C# and C++ developers. These certifications and courses can not only deepen your understanding of the languages but also demonstrate your commitment to continuous learning and professional growth.

Microsoft Certified Professional (MCP) - C#

As one of the most recognized certifications, MCP - C# validates your proficiency in C# programming and .NET framework. This certification is designed for developers seeking to build applications using C# and Visual Studio. The topics covered include language syntax, object-oriented programming, and data access with ADO.NET.

Microsoft Certified Solutions Developer (MCSD) - App Builder

This certification targets developers who want to showcase their skills in developing modern web and mobile applications using C# and other Microsoft technologies. Earning MCSD - App Builder demonstrates your ability to build advanced solutions on the Microsoft platform.

C++ Certified Professional Programmer (CPP)

Offered by the C++ Institute, the CPP certification is designed to test your C++ programming skills and understanding of essential concepts. It covers topics such as C++ syntax, data structures, and memory management. Earning this certification can be valuable, especially if you aim to work on complex C++ projects.

C++ Institute Certified Associate Programmer (CPA)

The CPA certification is an entry-level certification that evaluates your foundational knowledge of C++ programming. It's a suitable starting point for beginners looking to establish a strong base in C++ development.

Online Learning Platforms

In addition to certifications, numerous online learning platforms offer specialized courses in C# and C++. Platforms like Udemy, Pluralsight, Coursera, and edX host a wide array of courses catering to all levels of proficiency. These courses cover diverse topics, from C# web development to advanced C++ algorithms.

Importance of Certifications and How They Can Enhance Your Resume

Certifications hold significant value in the job market, particularly for C# and C++ developers. Here's how certifications can positively impact your resume and career:

Validation of Skills

Certifications provide tangible proof of your skills and knowledge in a specific area. Employers view certified candidates as professionals who have demonstrated their abilities through standardized assessments.

Increased Employability

Having relevant certifications can make you stand out among other job applicants. It shows that you are committed to continuous learning and are proactive in keeping up with industry trends.

Career Advancement

Certifications can open doors to new job opportunities and career advancement. They may be a deciding factor in promotions or salary negotiations, as employers often value certified professionals.

Demonstrating Expertise

Acquiring specialized certifications demonstrates your expertise in a particular domain, such as web development, game development, or database management.

Personal Growth

Preparing for certifications and completing courses can broaden your knowledge and challenge you to explore new concepts and best practices.

When pursuing certifications and courses, it's essential to select ones that align with your career goals and interests. Additionally, actively participating in projects and contributing to open-source communities can complement your certifications, showcasing your practical abilities and teamwork skills.

Chapter 3: Essential Skills for C# and C++ Developers

Review of the Skill Set Required for Proficient C# and C++ Developers

Becoming a proficient C# and C++ developer requires a diverse skill set that goes beyond knowing the syntax of the languages. In this chapter, we will delve into the fundamental skills that are crucial for successful C# and C++ development:

Strong Understanding of Object-Oriented Programming (OOP)

Object-oriented programming is the foundation of both C# and C++. Developers must grasp key OOP concepts such as classes, objects, inheritance, polymorphism, and encapsulation. OOP enables developers to design efficient and maintainable code, making it an essential skill for building complex software systems.

Memory Management

In C++, manual memory management is a critical aspect of the language. Developers should have a deep understanding of memory allocation and deallocation to avoid memory leaks and optimize resource utilization. C# developers should also be familiar with the garbage collection process and how to manage object lifetimes.

Proficiency in Algorithms and Data Structures

A strong grasp of algorithms and data structures is vital for solving problems efficiently. This skill is particularly important for C++ developers working on performance-critical applications, such as games or high-performance software.

Knowledge of the .NET Framework

For C# developers, a comprehensive understanding of the .NET Framework is crucial. The framework provides a wide range of libraries and APIs that simplify development tasks. Proficient C# developers leverage these resources effectively to build robust and feature-rich applications.

Multithreading and Concurrency

Modern applications often require handling multiple tasks concurrently. Proficient developers should be well-versed in multithreading concepts and techniques to ensure thread safety and avoid race conditions.

Problem-Solving and Debugging Skills

Debugging is an integral part of the development process. C# and C++ developers must possess strong problem-solving skills and the ability to identify and resolve issues efficiently.

Techniques for Improving and Mastering These Skills

Improving and mastering the essential skills for C# and C++ development requires dedication, practice, and a growth mindset. Here are some techniques to enhance your expertise:

Hands-on Coding Projects

Engage in hands-on coding projects that challenge you to apply the concepts you learn. Working on real-world projects will deepen your understanding and improve your problem-solving skills.

Open-Source Contributions

Contributing to open-source projects allows you to collaborate with other developers and gain exposure to industry best practices. It also provides opportunities to learn from experienced programmers.

Online Tutorials and Resources

Leverage online tutorials, documentation, and resources from reputable sources like Microsoft Docs, C++ Reference, and Stack Overflow. These platforms offer a wealth of knowledge and solutions to common programming challenges.

Code Reviews and Feedback

Seek feedback from experienced developers through code reviews or online programming communities. Constructive criticism helps identify areas for improvement and provides valuable insights.

Continuous Learning

Stay updated with the latest trends, technologies, and best practices in C# and C++. Attend workshops, webinars, and conferences to expand your knowledge.

Collaborate on Team Projects

Collaborating with a diverse team of developers exposes you to different perspectives and workflows. It hones your communication skills and prepares you for real-world development environments.

Chapter 4: C# and C++ in the Job Market

Discussion on the Job Market for C# and C++ Developers

The job market for C# and C++ developers is vibrant and offers a wide range of opportunities across various industries. Both languages have a strong presence in the software development industry, making them valuable skills for aspiring programmers. Let's explore the job market landscape for C# and C++ developers:

Demand for C# and C++ Developers

The demand for C# and C++ developers remains steady due to the popularity and widespread use of these languages. C# is particularly prevalent in the development of Windows applications, web applications using ASP.NET, and game development using Unity. On the other hand, C++ is widely used in performance-critical applications like games, embedded systems, and high-performance software.

Industries Hiring C# and C++ Developers

C# and C++ developers are sought after in a variety of industries. In the technology sector, you can find opportunities in software development companies, gaming studios, and IT consulting firms. Additionally, industries like finance, automotive, aerospace, and manufacturing often require C++ developers for their performance-driven applications.

Job Roles for C# and C++ Developers

The job roles for C# and C++ developers can vary based on the industry and project requirements. Some common job titles include Software Developer, Application Developer, Game Developer, Systems Developer, and Embedded Systems Engineer.

Skills in Demand

In addition to C# and C++ proficiency, employers look for developers with knowledge of relevant frameworks, libraries, and tools. For C# developers, skills in ASP.NET, .NET Core, Entity Framework, and Xamarin are often desirable. For C++ developers, experience with game engines like Unreal Engine or middleware libraries like Boost can be advantageous.

Remote Work Opportunities

The COVID-19 pandemic has accelerated the adoption of remote work, making it more common for C# and C++ developers to work remotely. This flexibility opens up opportunities with companies worldwide.

Tips for Finding and Applying to Relevant Jobs

Finding and applying to relevant C# and C++ jobs requires a strategic approach and effective job search techniques. Here are some tips to enhance your job search:

1. Build a Strong Portfolio: Create a portfolio showcasing your projects, contributions to open-source projects, and any relevant work experience. A portfolio helps employers assess your skills and contributions.

2. Utilize Job Search Platforms: Explore job search platforms like LinkedIn, Indeed, Glassdoor, and specialized tech job boards to find relevant opportunities. Set up job alerts to receive notifications for new openings.

3. Network and Attend Events: Attend tech meetups, workshops, and industry events to network with professionals and potential employers. Networking can lead to valuable job referrals and insights into the job market.

4. Tailor Your Resume and Cover Letter: Customize your resume and cover letter for each job application. Highlight your C# and C++ skills, relevant projects, and any industry-specific experience that aligns with the job requirements.

5. Prepare for Interviews: Practice coding exercises, algorithms, and C# or C++ concepts to be well-prepared for technical interviews. Research the company and be ready to discuss how your skills align with their projects and goals.

6. Continuous Learning: Stay updated with the latest advancements in C# and C++. Continuous learning demonstrates your commitment to professional growth and can set you apart from other candidates.

Chapter 5: Interviews and Resume Building for C# and C++ Developers

Techniques for Building an Impressive Resume and Performing Well in Interviews

Your resume and interview performance play a crucial role in landing a job as a C# or C++ developer. A well-crafted resume showcases your skills and experience, while a successful interview highlights your technical proficiency and communication abilities. Let's explore techniques to create an impressive resume and excel in interviews:

Crafting Your Resume

- Highlight Relevant Skills: Tailor your resume to emphasize C# and C++ skills and any related technologies or frameworks you have worked with. Use specific examples and metrics to demonstrate your impact in previous projects.

- Showcase Projects: Include a section highlighting your notable projects. Describe the project's purpose, your role, and the technologies you used. Providing links to GitHub repositories or project demos can showcase your work in action.

- Certifications and Courses: Mention any relevant certifications or courses you have completed. These demonstrate your commitment to professional development and can be a valuable addition to your resume.

- Keep It Concise: Avoid excessive length. A one-page or two-page resume is generally sufficient, but ensure all important information is included.

Preparing for Interviews

- Review Core Concepts: Brush up on fundamental C# and C++ concepts, data structures, algorithms, and design patterns. Be prepared to discuss how you've applied them in your previous projects.

- Practice Coding: Practicing coding challenges and whiteboard exercises will improve your problem-solving skills and help you tackle technical interviews confidently.

- Communication Skills: Work on articulating your ideas clearly and concisely. Practice explaining technical concepts to non-technical interviewers.

- Research the Company: Learn about the company, its projects, and its culture. Tailor your answers to demonstrate how your skills align with their needs.

Case Studies and Examples of Successful Interviews and Resumes

A well-crafted resume and a strong performance during interviews are crucial for landing a job as a C# or C++ developer. In this chapter, we will delve into case studies and provide examples of successful interviews and resumes that have helped developers stand out in the competitive job market. Let's explore the strategies employed by these individuals to make a lasting impression on potential employers.

Case Study: John's Resume Success

John, an aspiring C++ developer, created a resume that showcased both his technical skills and problem-solving abilities. His resume followed a clean and professional format, with clear headings and concise descriptions of his projects and achievements.

Key Points

- John started with a strong summary that highlighted his passion for C++ programming and his experience with relevant technologies.

- He listed his technical skills, ensuring that keywords such as C++, STL, and Boost were included.

- John described his key projects in detail, emphasizing the challenges he faced and how he overcame them using C++ concepts and libraries.

- He included links to GitHub repositories showcasing his code and contributions to open-source projects.

Outcome

John's resume impressed employers, and he received several interview invitations. During the interviews, he could confidently discuss his projects and demonstrate his problem-solving abilities. This led to multiple job offers, enabling him to choose the best-fitting position.

Case Study: Sarah's Interview Success

Sarah, a C# developer with limited professional experience, prepared extensively for her interviews. Despite her lack of work experience, she highlighted her passion for C# development and her commitment to continuous learning.

Key Points

- Sarah researched the companies she was interviewing with and tailored her answers to match their projects and values.
- She practiced coding exercises and algorithms regularly to enhance her problem-solving skills.
- Sarah showcased her personal projects and how they aligned with the company's tech stack and goals.
- During interviews, she emphasized her willingness to learn and adapt to new technologies.

Outcome

Sarah's thorough preparation and genuine interest in C# development made a positive impact on interviewers. Even without substantial work experience, her passion and dedication to learning stood out. As a result, she secured an entry-level position at a tech company that values growth potential.

Case Study: Michael's Behavioral Interview Approach

Michael, a seasoned C++ developer, was well-versed in technical concepts but wanted to excel in behavioral interviews. He focused on conveying his communication skills, teamwork, and ability to handle challenges effectively.

Key Points

- Michael practiced answering common behavioral interview questions, such as how he resolved conflicts with team members or handled tight deadlines.

- He used the STAR method (Situation, Task, Action, Result) to structure his responses, making them clear and concise.

- Michael provided real-life examples from his previous work experiences to demonstrate his skills in action.

Outcome

Michael's approach to behavioral interviews impressed potential employers, as it showcased his ability to collaborate and handle real-world scenarios. This, combined with his strong technical expertise, led to offers from companies looking for developers who could excel in both technical and soft skills.

Chapter 6: Industry Trends for C# and C++: What's Coming Next?

In-depth Exploration of the Latest Trends in the C# and C++ Industries

The technology landscape is constantly evolving, and the worlds of C# and C++ development are no exceptions. In this chapter, we will dive into the current trends and emerging technologies that are shaping the future of these programming languages. As developers, staying updated with the latest industry trends is crucial for career growth and staying relevant in the fast-paced tech industry.

Cross-Platform Development

One of the significant trends in both the C# and C++ industries is the increasing emphasis on cross-platform development. With the rise of mobile devices and different operating systems, developers are seeking ways to write code that can be deployed across multiple platforms seamlessly. C# developers can leverage frameworks like Xamarin to build native mobile applications for iOS and Android, while C++ developers can use tools like Qt to create cross-platform applications with a native look and feel.

Performance Optimization

As software demands continue to grow, performance optimization remains a top priority for C# and C++ developers. The demand for high-performance applications that consume fewer resources has led to advancements in compiler technologies and runtime environments. Developers are exploring techniques such as multithreading, parallel processing, and low-level optimizations to achieve the best performance for their applications.

IoT and Embedded Systems

Both C# and C++ play essential roles in the Internet of Things (IoT) and embedded systems development. C++ is widely used in resource-constrained environments due to its efficiency and low-level capabilities. On the other hand, C# is gaining traction in the IoT space with platforms like .NET IoT Core, enabling developers to build IoT solutions using familiar C# libraries and frameworks.

AI and Machine Learning

Artificial Intelligence (AI) and Machine Learning (ML) are transforming various industries, and C# and C++ are not lagging behind in this domain. C++ is often chosen for implementing computationally intensive algorithms and real-time processing in ML applications, while C# with libraries like ML.NET enables developers to build ML models and integrate AI capabilities into their applications.

Cloud Computing and Microservices

The adoption of cloud computing and microservices architecture is rapidly increasing, and C# and C++ developers are leveraging these technologies to build scalable and resilient applications. C# developers can harness the power of Microsoft Azure, while C++ developers can use cloud libraries and SDKs to interact with cloud services.

Blockchain Development

With the growing interest in blockchain technology, C++ is a favored language for building blockchain-based applications and cryptocurrencies. Its ability to handle low-level memory management and computational efficiency makes it ideal for this niche.

Quantum Computing

While still in its early stages, quantum computing is a promising technology that could revolutionize computing capabilities. C# and C++ have started exploring quantum development frameworks like Microsoft Quantum Development Kit, preparing developers for the future of quantum computing.

The Importance of Staying Current with C# and C++ Updates

In the ever-changing landscape of software development, staying current with the latest updates, trends, and advancements is crucial for C# and C++ developers. Both C# and C++ are widely used programming languages, and their popularity is expected to grow as technology continues to advance. As developers, it is essential to remain up-to-date with the latest changes and improvements in these languages to remain competitive in the job market and maximize career opportunities.

Leveraging New Features and Enhancements

Both C# and C++ receive regular updates that introduce new features, enhancements, and optimizations. Staying current with these updates allows developers to leverage the latest language features and take advantage of performance improvements. By incorporating these advancements into their codebase, developers can create more efficient, maintainable, and robust applications.

Ensuring Compatibility

Technology evolves rapidly, and new hardware and software platforms are constantly being introduced. By staying current with C# and C++ updates, developers can ensure their applications remain compatible with the latest platforms, operating systems, and frameworks. This is especially important for developers working on cross-platform applications, as staying up-to-date ensures seamless deployment and functionality across various devices and environments.

Security and Bug Fixes

Software security is of paramount importance, and vulnerabilities are regularly identified in programming languages and frameworks. Keeping C# and C++ up-to-date ensures that developers have access to the latest security patches and bug fixes, reducing the risk of potential security breaches. Additionally, using older versions of programming languages may expose applications to compatibility issues and performance bottlenecks.

Adapting to Industry Needs

As new technologies and industry trends emerge, developers who are up-to-date with C# and C++ updates can quickly adapt to changing market demands. For instance, being familiar with the latest updates can help developers transition to new platforms, frameworks, or industries that require specialized knowledge of C# and C++.

Career Growth and Employability

Staying current with C# and C++ updates enhances a developer's skillset and makes them more desirable to employers. Companies seek developers who can bring the latest knowledge and expertise to their projects. Additionally, being well-versed in the latest language updates can open doors to new job opportunities and career advancements.

Contributing to Open Source Projects

Many C# and C++ projects are open source, and the developer community regularly contributes to these projects. Staying current with language updates allows developers to actively contribute to the development and improvement of the languages and libraries, fostering a collaborative and supportive community.

Continued Learning and Growth

Programming languages like C# and C++ are continuously evolving, and keeping up with updates is an excellent way for developers to engage in lifelong learning. Embracing new concepts and technologies not only keeps developers competitive but also provides a sense of fulfillment and growth in their careers.

Advice on Preparing for Changes and New Advancements in C# and C++

As the software development landscape continues to evolve rapidly, it is essential for C# and C++ developers to stay ahead of the curve and be prepared for the changes and new advancements in these programming languages. Embracing the latest industry trends and technologies not only enhances career prospects but also enables developers to build innovative and efficient applications. Here are some valuable pieces of advice to help C# and C++ developers prepare for what's coming next:

Stay Informed and Curious

The world of technology is constantly changing, and new trends and advancements emerge regularly. To stay prepared, it is crucial for developers to remain informed and curious about the latest developments in C# and C++. Follow reputable blogs, forums, and official announcements to stay up-to-date with language updates, new features, and best practices.

Continuous Learning

Learning should be an ongoing process in any developer's career. Attend conferences, webinars, and workshops to gain insights into upcoming industry trends and techniques. Consider enrolling in online courses or participating in coding bootcamps that focus on C# and C++ to expand your knowledge and skills.

Embrace New Frameworks and Libraries

The C# and C++ ecosystems are constantly evolving, with new frameworks and libraries being introduced regularly. Developers should be open to exploring and adopting new technologies to enhance their development capabilities and build more powerful applications.

Join Developer Communities

Engaging with developer communities, both online and offline, is a great way to stay connected with industry trends. Participate in discussion forums, GitHub repositories, and developer meetups to network with like-minded professionals and share knowledge.

Develop Problem-Solving Skills

The ability to solve complex problems efficiently is invaluable for C# and C++ developers. Regularly engage in coding challenges, algorithms, and data structure problems to sharpen your problem-solving skills and improve code efficiency.

Maintain a Versatile Skillset

While specializing in C# or C++ is valuable, being proficient in related technologies and languages can make developers more adaptable to changing industry needs. Familiarity with web development, database management, or mobile app development can complement C# and C++ skills.

Collaborate and Network

Building connections with fellow developers, mentors, and industry professionals can lead to new opportunities and insights. Networking can provide valuable feedback, guidance, and even potential job offers.

Balance Practical Experience with Theory

While learning theory is essential, practical experience is equally crucial. Work on personal projects and collaborate on real-world applications to apply the knowledge gained in practical scenarios.

Be Adaptable and Agile

The tech industry is known for its fast-paced nature. Developers who are adaptable and agile in learning new technologies and methodologies are better equipped to thrive in the ever-changing landscape.

Chapter 7: Continuing Your Programming Journey: Further Learning and Development

Preparing for Continued Self-Learning and Development in C# and C++

In the fast-paced world of software development, continuous learning and personal development are essential for C# and C++ developers to stay relevant, advance their careers, and tackle new challenges effectively. Chapter 7 explores the importance of ongoing learning and provides valuable guidance on how to prepare for continued self-improvement in C# and C++. Embracing a growth mindset and committing to lifelong learning will enable developers to thrive in this ever-evolving field.

Set Clear Goals

Before diving into further learning, it's crucial to establish clear goals. Determine the specific areas of C# and C++ that interest you the most or align with your career aspirations. Whether it's mastering specific frameworks, enhancing debugging skills, or exploring new design patterns, having well-defined goals will guide your learning journey.

Identify Learning Resources

There are numerous learning resources available for C# and C++ developers, ranging from books, online tutorials, and courses to community forums and coding challenges. Identify reputable sources that suit your learning style and preferences, and don't hesitate to explore a variety of materials.

Online Learning Platforms

Online learning platforms such as Coursera, Udemy, Pluralsight, and Codecademy offer a vast array of C# and C++ courses designed to cater to all levels of expertise. Enroll in courses that match your goals and interests, and work through them systematically.

Work on Real-World Projects

Applying the knowledge gained through hands-on projects is one of the most effective ways to reinforce learning. Consider contributing to open-source projects, building your personal projects, or collaborating with peers to solve real-world challenges.

Follow Industry Trends

Stay updated with the latest trends, tools, and best practices in C# and C++. Regularly follow tech blogs, podcasts, and attend conferences and webinars to gain insights into emerging technologies and methodologies.

Join Online Communities

Participate in C# and C++ developer communities to interact with like-minded individuals, share knowledge, and seek advice from experienced professionals. Engaging with others can provide valuable feedback and foster collaborative learning.

Practice Regularly

Consistent practice is key to retaining knowledge and honing skills. Dedicate time each week to practice coding exercises, algorithm problems, and exploring new features of C# and C++.

Attend Workshops and Meetups

Participate in workshops and meetups to gain hands-on experience, learn from experts, and network with potential employers and colleagues.

Embrace Challenges

Learning and development involve overcoming challenges. Embrace the occasional frustration and setbacks as part of the learning process, and use them as opportunities to grow.

Resources and Advice for Ongoing Development and Learning

Continuing your programming journey in C# and C++ involves a commitment to lifelong learning and embracing opportunities for personal and professional growth. In this section, we explore a wealth of resources and provide valuable advice to empower developers with the tools they need to expand their knowledge and skill set. These resources will not only help developers stay up-to-date with the latest advancements in C# and C++ but also equip them to tackle complex challenges and excel in their careers.

1. Online Learning Platforms

Online learning platforms like Coursera, Udemy, Pluralsight, and edX offer a wide range of courses on C# and C++. These courses can help you learn new concepts, deepen your understanding of the languages, and stay up-to-date with the latest features and best practices.

2. Books

Books are a great way to delve deep into a topic. Some recommended books for C# include "C# in Depth" by Jon Skeet and "Pro C# 7" by Andrew Troelsen. For C++, consider "Effective Modern C++" by Scott Meyers and "C++ Primer" by Stanley B. Lippman, Josée Lajoie, and Barbara E. Moo.

3. Documentation and Official Websites

The official documentation for both C# (.NET Docs) and C++ (cppreference.com) are excellent resources. They provide comprehensive and up-to-date information about the languages, including tutorials, guides, and reference materials.

4. Coding Practice Websites

Websites like LeetCode, HackerRank, and CodeSignal offer coding challenges that can help you practice your C# and C++ skills. These challenges range from easy to hard and cover a wide range of topics, making them a good way to practice and learn.

5. Open Source Projects

Contributing to open source projects can be a great way to learn and grow. It allows you to work on real-world projects, collaborate with other developers, and learn from their code. Websites like GitHub and GitLab host a vast number of open source projects.

6. Blogs and Podcasts

Blogs like the .NET Blog and ISO C++ Blog, and podcasts like CppCast and .NET Rocks, can help you stay up-to-date with the latest news, trends, and best practices in C# and C++.

7. Meetups and Conferences

Attending meetups and conferences can help you connect with other developers, learn from experts, and stay informed about the latest developments in the field. Websites like Meetup.com can help you find local events.

The journey of a C# and C++ developer doesn't end with a single book. Instead, it opens the door to a world of endless possibilities. By utilizing the resources and advice provided in this chapter, developers can continue their programming journey, embracing lifelong learning, and thriving in the ever-evolving landscape of technology. Whether it's exploring online courses, contributing to open-source projects, staying updated with industry trends, or seeking mentorship, the path to success lies in consistent dedication to learning and development. Embrace these resources and let them guide you towards an exciting and rewarding career in C# and C++.

References

Book 1 - C# Programming: The Essential Guide for Beginners

1. Albahari, J., & Albahari, B. (2020). C# 9.0 in a Nutshell: The Definitive Reference. O'Reilly Media.
2. Miles, R. (2020). C# Programming Yellow Book.
3. Coursera: Offers C# courses. https://www.coursera.org/
4. Pluralsight. (n.d.). C# Learning Paths. Retrieved from https://www.pluralsight.com/
5. Udemy: C# Programming Courses. https://www.udemy.com/topic/c-sharp/
6. Reddit C# Community. Retrieved from https://www.reddit.com/r/csharp/
7. Stack Overflow. (n.d.). A popular Q&A community for programming. https://stackoverflow.com/
8. Microsoft Docs. (n.d.). Official documentation for C# and .NET. Retrieved from https://docs.microsoft.com/en-us/dotnet/csharp/

Book 2 - C# Programming: Intermediate Techniques and Frameworks

1. Explore open-source C# projects on GitHub. https://github.com/topics/csharp
2. Freeman, A., & Ross, K. (2017). Head First C#: A Learner's Guide to Real-World Programming with C#, XAML, and .NET. O'Reilly Media.
3. Brackeys: Provides game development tutorials in C#. https://www.youtube.com/user/Brackeys

Book 3 - C# Programming: Advanced Concepts and Industry Practices

1. Lippert, E. (2010). C# Secrets: Double-Check Locking and the Singleton Pattern. MSDN Magazine, 25(6).
2. Ostrovsky, I. (2012). C# - The C# Memory Model in Theory and Practice. MSDN Magazine, 27(12). https://msdn.microsoft.com/en-us/magazine/jj863136.aspx

Book 4 - C++ Programming: A Practical Introduction

1. Coursera: Offers C++ courses. https://www.coursera.org/
2. Pluralsight. (n.d.). C++ Learning Paths. Retrieved from https://www.pluralsight.com/
3. Udemy: C++ Programming Courses. https://www.udemy.com/

4. cppreference.com. (n.d.). Comprehensive C++ reference and documentation. https://en.cppreference.com/w/

5. Reddit C++ Community. https://www.reddit.com/r/cpp/

6. Stack Overflow. (n.d.). A popular Q&A community for programming. https://stackoverflow.com/

Book 5 - C++ Programming: Mastering Complex Structures and Database Management

1. Stroustrup, B. (2013). The C++ Programming Language (4th ed.). Addison-Wesley Professional.

2. Meyers, S. (2014). Effective Modern C++: 42 Specific Ways to Improve Your Use of C++11 and C++14. O'Reilly Media.

3. Sutter, H. (2005). The Free Lunch Is Over: A Fundamental Turn Toward Concurrency in Software. Dr. Dobb's Journal, 30(3). Retrieved from http://www.gotw.ca/publications/concurrency-ddj.htm

4. The Cherno. (n.d.). C++ Game Development Tutorials. Retrieved from https://www.youtube.com/user/TheChernoProject

5. Lippman, S. B., Lajoie, J., & Moo, B. E. (2012). C++ Primer (5th ed.). Addison-Wesley Professional.

Book 6 - C# and C++: Bridging the Gap

1. LeetCode. (n.d.). Practice C# and C++ Coding Questions. https://leetcode.com/

2. HackerRank. (n.d.). C# and C++ Practice. https://www.hackerrank.com/

3. Pluralsight: Courses on C# and C++ integration. https://www.pluralsight.com/

4. Reddit Communities: Discussions on C# and C++ integration. https://www.reddit.com/

Book 7 - C# and C++: Career Preparation and Beyond

1. Glassdoor: C# and C++ job listings and company reviews. https://www.glassdoor.com/Community/index.htm

2. LinkedIn: Networking and job opportunities for C# and C++ developers. https://www.linkedin.com/

3. Reddit Communities: Career advice for C# and C++ developers. https://www.reddit.com/

Printed in Great Britain
by Amazon